MW01102423

Julie & Lawrie McEn

COMPLETE BOOK OF
FISHING
BAITS
& RIGS

TEXT BY
JULIE & LAWRIE McENALLY

ILLUSTRATIONS BY
GEOFF WILSON

PHOTOGRAPHY BY
JULIE & LAWRIE McENALLY
GEOFF WILSON & BILL CLASSON

EDITOR & CONSULTANT
BILL CLASSON

DESIGN & PRODUCTION
GLENDA ROACH

PRINTING BY
Southern Lithographics Pty. Ltd. (Melbourne)

International Copyright 1995 by Australian Fishing Network.

All rights reserved.

Published and Distributed by
Australian Fishing Network

AFN
AUSTRALIAN FISHING NETWORK

Book *of baits*

Forword

Using a baited hook to catch a fish is as old as man-kind. It is a simple act aimed at inducing a fish to eat a bait containing a hook and then securing the fish with the hook.

For anyone learning about fishing, baiting a hook is a key part of their fishing knowledge. For experienced anglers there is an endless learning curve to be navigated, seeking new methods and techniques to improve captures.

This book is aimed at showing anglers how to catch, find or make the bait and how it should be presented to the fish for best results. The rigs necessary for good presentation are also included.

The real secret of catching fish on bait is to keep everything as natural and as simple as possible. The baits and rigs used in this publication follow that principle closely.

The key to good results is premium bait, presented in a natural manner that the fish want to eat. At this point the angler has done everything possible, the rest is up to the fish.

This is the very essence of angling, get it right and better catches will certainly follow.

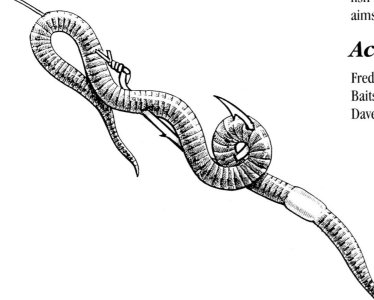

Introduction

Producing a guide to baits and rigs is not something that happens overnight. This book is a compilation of three decades of fishing experience squeezed into 80 pages.

There is much to learn about the many facets of bait and this book aims to give anglers the benefit of experience. Learning from anglers who have done much of the hard work makes things easier and faster for those who want to learn the craft or just improve their angling skills.

Having good bait is one of the real keys to productive fishing. Sometimes the bait can be as hard to catch as the fish being sought. Sometimes it can be purchased, otherwise, the angler has to catch the bait and keep it alive for later use. It is all part of the challenge of being a good angler.

Some forms of bait catching are just plain hard work. Digging bloodworms and pumping nippers being prime examples. While catching baits like beach-worms, takes real skill. Often it is just a matter of catching one fish so that another fish can eat it. Whatever bait is being sought, catching or finding natural or live baits takes some sort of work or skill to ensure the supply for the fishing which follows.

By taking a little extra care when selecting, buying, catching and using baits most anglers will catch more fish or catch fish more regularly. Either way this book aims to improve the fishing enjoyment of all anglers.

Acknowledgments

Fred Jobson, Freshwater Baits, Bill Classon, Freshwater Baits, Geoff Wilson, Illustrations, Nathan Falla and Dave Payne, Bait Collection.

contents

4 Bardi Grubs
6 Cockles: Pipis & Goolwa
8 Crabs
10 Crickets & Grasshoppers
12 Cunjevoi
14 Cut Baits
16 Cuttlefish
18 Flour Baits: Bread, Dough & Pudding
20 Garfish
22 Gutbaits
24 Hardyheads
26 Herrings
28 Mackerel: Slimy
30 Minnows: Galaxids, Gudgeons & Smelt
32 Mudeyes
34 Mullet
36 Mussels
38 Octopus
40 Pilchards
42 Prawns
44 Razorfish
44 Shrimp: Pistol
46 Shrimp: Estuary
48 Shrimp: Freshwater
50 Squid
52 Tuna: Small
58 Weeds: Cabbage & Green
56 Whitebait & Frogmouth
58 Worms: Beach
60 Worms: Blood
62 Worms: Garden & Red Wriggler
64 Worms: Sand & Wriggler
66 Worms: Scrub
68 Yabbies: Freshwater
70 Yabbies: Saltwater
72 Yellowtail
74 Bait Jig Rigs
76 Presentation is the Key
78 Bait Collecting Gear

Bardi*grubs*

Yellowbelly and Murray cod are keenly attracted to bardi grubs.

Bardi grubs are the larvae of a large moth and are an uniquely Australian bait. While no bait will catch fish all the time, the big, fat, creamy bardi grubs found along the plains of the inland rivers are about the closest thing to it for inland native fish. The grubs are collected by both recreational anglers and professional bait gatherers and given the numbers collected they are obviously a prolific insect.

Finding and catching the grub is not easy and is a skill learned by being shown a few of the tricks of the trade. For most anglers the easy way out is to buy the grubs.

This is often the best answer if time is short, but if fishing in an area where the grubs are common, catching them can be an interesting diversion.

Where to Find Them

Bardi grubs are found in the ground under the exposed roots of red gums and grey box trees. The location of favoured bardi grub areas is usually a well kept secret and some trial and error may be involved.

The favoured trees are usually spaced with clear pasture beneath and a powdery layer of grey looking soil over friable but packed sandy clay. This top layer is usually from 75 to 100 mm thick but may be up to 300 mm thick.

Shifting this layer with a shovel reveals a hard, compacted surface of clay with the holes of the bardi grubs showing clearly.

How to Catch Them

Getting the grub out of the burrow is the hard part. In the past, a length of reed with a knot tied in the end was inserted down the hole. This irritated the grub into biting the straw and it hopefully would be whisked out before it let go.

Now a device is available to allow the grub to be readily caught without damage

How to Use Them

The grubs are placed on a hook by feeding the point of the hook into the tail and then pushing the grub around the bend of the hook until the whole hook is just about in the grub.

The point of the hook is then pushed out of the grub on its underside. Gripping the point of the hook with the thumb and forefinger the eye of the hook is then drawn into the grub. By doing this, the grub is virtually locked onto the hook by having the eye of the hook inside the tough, leathery skin. This keeps the bait securely fastened during casting.

Hook sizes should be appropriate to both the size of the bait and the fish being sought. On trout, the smaller size grubs seem to work best with hooks in the No.4 to 1/0 size.

On cod and yellowbelly something in the 1/0 to 4/0 range is appropriate although larger hooks may be selected if big baits are being used and large cod are expected.

The best rigs depend on the area being fished. Because the grubs are quite heavy they can be fished without a sinker in dams and impoundments, although most anglers use a running ball sinker to add casting weight and to help position the bait. The same rig is also popular with river anglers who use slightly heavier ball sinkers to compensate for the strength of the current.

Yellowbelly anglers often use a paternoster rig with the sinker on the bottom and two hooks on droppers standing off the main line.

Alternatively, a simple estuary type rig with the hook joined to the swivel by a 35 cm trace and a running sinker is also quite effective.

Profile of bardi grubs with one hooked through the body with point extending clearly underneath.

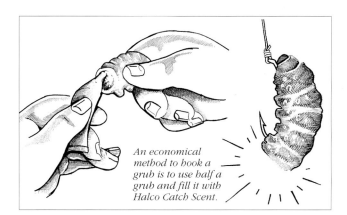

An economical method to hook a grub is to use half a grub and fill it with Halco Catch Scent.

and with few problems. This device consists of a speedo or bike brake cable with three metal fingers on the end threaded with a loop of heavy monofilament line.

This cable slides down the hole until the three metal fingers slip over the head of the grub. The line is then pulled tight via the monofilament which runs the whole length of the probe. The arms close firmly around the head of the grub and it is pulled from its burrow unharmed.

For anyone interested, the probes are available from Hunter Marine in Swan Hill in Victoria (Ph. 050 322320).

Handling

Bardi grubs handle easily and the only key is to not injure them during capture. The grubs can be kept in the timber and sawdust of the tree in which they were found.

Like any insect they can be held in 'suspended animation' by refrigerating them at cool but not extremely cold temperatures. In this state they will use little or no energy and will last six weeks or more.

Points of Note

While there is a defined animal known as the bardi grub, there are plenty of other beetle and moth larvae that can be successfully used as bait. Most freshwater fish find these rich, juicy grubs to their taste and using any grubs in this category is worthwhile.

Murray cod are often caught on bardi grubs in both rivers and lakes.

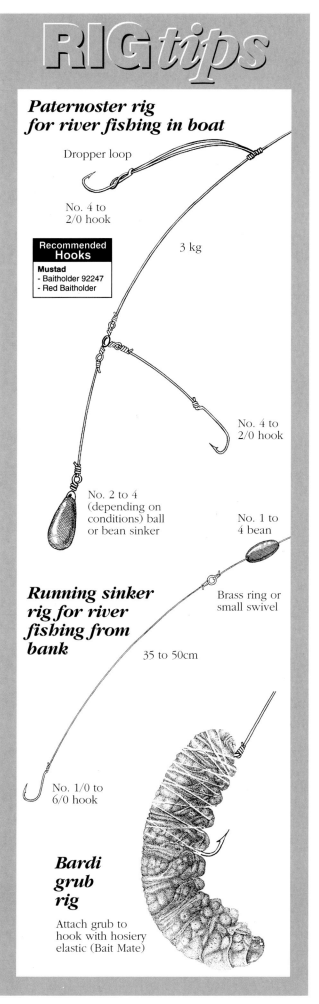

Paternoster rig for river fishing in boat

Dropper loop

No. 4 to 2/0 hook

Recommended Hooks
Mustad
- Baitholder 92247
- Red Baitholder

3 kg

No. 4 to 2/0 hook

No. 2 to 4 (depending on conditions) ball or bean sinker

No. 1 to 4 bean

Brass ring or small swivel

Running sinker rig for river fishing from bank

35 to 50cm

No. 1/0 to 6/0 hook

Bardi grub rig

Attach grub to hook with hosiery elastic (Bait Mate)

Cockles *pipis & goolwa*

The most common bivalve of any size inhabiting the sand of many ocean beaches is *Donax deltoides* or pipi as it is commonly known in New South Wales. This bivalve is also known as 'wong' on Fraser Island, 'eugari' in southern Queensland, cockles in Victoria and Goolwa cockles in South Australia.

It is a large bivalve, the smooth outer surface of which varies from a tinted white, through yellow to a

Pipis or Goolwa cockles on beach.

Once found pipis can often be collected in numbers.

blue-purple in colour. It has a strong 'tongue' or 'foot' which it uses to move around in the sand and for burrowing back into the sand.

These bivalve molluscs are a top bait for a wide range of surf and estuary fish and can be easily gathered from many ocean beaches.

Because these shellfish are easy to gather and have been over harvested in many places, bag limits now exist on the number that can be collected by recreational anglers. Check with the local Fisheries office for details. Pipis are very good baits for catching bream, trevally, whiting, particularly King George whiting, leatherjackets and many others.

Where to Find Them

Pipis are abundant between the high and low tide marks on beaches right around the eastern and southern coastline of the continent. They are most common on long, deserted beaches which are not continually worked over by bait seeking anglers and commercial gatherers.

They are easiest to find at the lower part of the tide when the water has receded sufficiently to allow access to the most likely areas. Generally, pipis live just a few centimetres below the surface but on occasions can be seen being knocked around by the waves. The shoulder areas of beach sand ridges are usually the best places to start looking. Collecting is done by probing the sand with the feet.

How to Use Them

The pipi is opened by inserting a knife at the narrowest point and twisting. This will expose the shellfish which is easily removed and can be used either whole or sliced into bait sized pieces.

When slicing them into smaller pieces always ensure that part of the foot or tongue is included in each slice, this is essential for keeping the bait on the hook.

Most anglers use the whole shellfish by placing the hook through the foot or tongue and either threading or sliding all the hook into the bait. This will stay firmly in place for casting and hold together well when eaten by the fish.

Open pipi with rigged bait. Note the hook is always placed in the firm tongue of the pipi.

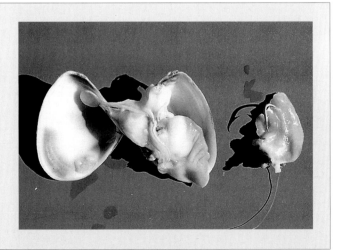

How to Catch Them

Stand in the active surf area in the swash zone, which is where the waves wash up and down the beach and twist both feet as the water moves in and out.

As soon as you notice a hard object under foot, keep pressure on it and gather it by hand. Once one pipi is found there are usually others nearby.

Always carry a bucket or shoulder pack to drop the pipis into rather than having to walk up and down the beach with each handful.

Handling

Pipis can be kept alive for several days in a wet sugar bag in a cool, shady spot or in aerated sea water which needs to be changed daily.

Points of Note

Pipis make excellent berley as well as bait. The reason for this is they sink fast and remain in the fishing area, they are extremely attractive to the fish and they can be broken up so the fish have to work at them to get at the contents.

They are also a cheap and relatively abundant shellfish for both bait and berley.

To use them as berley just crush them with a pair of pliers and drop them over the side of the boat or throw them into the area being fished.

Any fish in the area will soon be drawn into the fishing zone by the smell of the smashed shellfish. Baits of similar shellfish fished in the same patch will soon be found by feeding fish.

Don't overdo the berley. Half a dozen shellfish first up will start things, followed by one or two freshly crushed shellfish every five or ten minutes until the fish start biting freely.

Dart and other surf fish are keen pipi feeders.

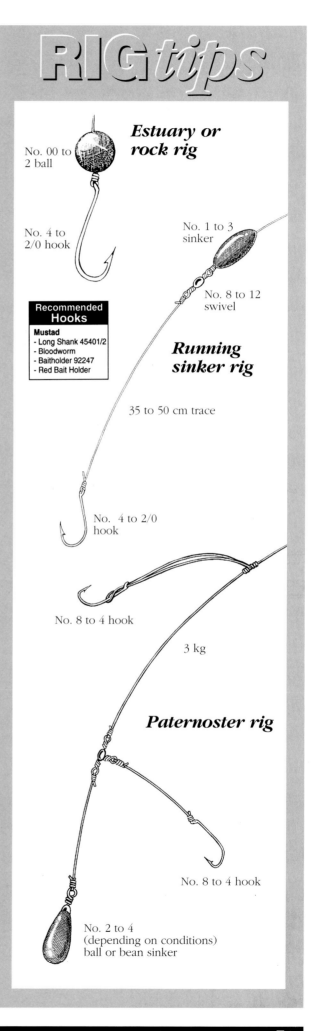

RIG*tips*

No. 00 to 2 ball

No. 4 to 2/0 hook

Estuary or rock rig

No. 1 to 3 sinker

No. 8 to 12 swivel

Recommended Hooks

Mustad
- Long Shank 45401/2
- Bloodworm
- Baitholder 92247
- Red Bait Holder

Running sinker rig

35 to 50 cm trace

No. 4 to 2/0 hook

No. 8 to 4 hook

3 kg

Paternoster rig

No. 8 to 4 hook

No. 2 to 4 (depending on conditions) ball or bean sinker

Crabs

A selection of estuary shoreline crabs.

A big part of the mulloway's diet are crabs of all varieties.

Small crabs of any kind are one of the most under-utilised baits available to anglers. Anglers fishing from the ocean rocks regularly use crabs for drummer, bream, groper and snapper yet most estuary anglers rarely use crabs.

An observant eye and the time to look will show that crabs are a prolific dweller of the intertidal zone of all estuaries. Keen anglers will also regularly find crabs in the stomach contents of bream, flathead, whiting, tarwhine, mulloway, snapper and many other fish.

From an anglers point of view, crabs provide an easily collected bait source that fish will eat, so why not use them?

Where to Find Them

Crabs can be found in nearly every marine habitat but are easiest to catch around rocky shorelines, on sea walls, estuary mudflats or on the ocean rocks during low tide. Most crabs make good bait however both fish and fishermen seem to have their preferences.

In the estuaries, the small black crab found under shoreline rocks and near mangroves seems to be the most productive.

Whiting and bream anglers regularly use very small soldier crabs with considerable success. Soldier crabs can be found on sandy or muddy shores in coastal lagoons or estuaries marching in their thousands, and can be easily captured.

Ghost crabs which are very good bait for surf dwelling bream can be found around the sand dunes at the back of most beaches. Rock fishermen tend to favour the red crab caught in weedy pools or under ledges along the ocean rocks.

How to Use Them

Crabs are a hardy bait that stay on the hook when casting and look attractive if rigged correctly. Small crabs are mostly used whole by breaking off the back leg and pushing the hook through the hole into the body cavity and out through the back joint area of the crab. Larger crabs are cut in half and the back leg removed for placing the hook through the body section.

Try to use hook sizes to suit both the bait and the fish. Usually No.1 to No.2 is about right for most species caught using crabs for bait.

Crabs can be used whole or in pieces depending on bait size and the fish being sought.

How to Catch Them

Each type of crab takes a slightly different technique to catch but the end result usually boils down to grabbing them one way or another with the hand.

The black estuary crab is caught by lifting rocks and timber along the shoreline and grabbing the crabs as they scuttle away looking for shelter.

Soldier crabs in the very small sizes usually turn up while pumping nippers with a bait pump. Larger specimens can be run down

Turning over rocks on mud flats can produce crabs, pistol shrimp and worms.

can be grabbed by hand.

Be warned, all crabs can and will nip the unwary, while most do little more than pinch, the red rock crab can break the skin and cause a bit of pain.

Handling

Shoreline crabs are hardy creatures and keep easily in a bucket with some wet seaweed. Just make sure the bucket has very smooth sides or better still a lid as crabs are excellent climbers.

As with most baits, temperature control is vital so store the crabs in a cool spot and they will keep for several days.

Points of Note

While crabs are good bait, they don't work everywhere. The best places to use them for bait is where the fish expect to be looking or hunting for them. Along rocky foreshores, breakwalls, oyster leases and off the ocean rocks are ideal locations to use crabs.

Ghost crabs used off the beach are effective and they do catch big bream, particularly at night.

One point to remember is to only take enough crabs for your immediate needs. It is easy to clean out a crab population with over harvesting.

while they march across the flats.

Ghost crabs are caught around the high water mark and near beach dunes at night using a bright torch. They can also be caught by using a tin or bucket buried right up to the lip in the sand and baited with a fish head.

Red rock crabs are usually caught by hand or with a finely tyned spear. Look for them around weedy rock pools. They can be attracted to and will firmly grab a tough piece of fish on a length of line. Once holding and feeding on the bait they

Ghost crabs are used whole when fishing the beach.

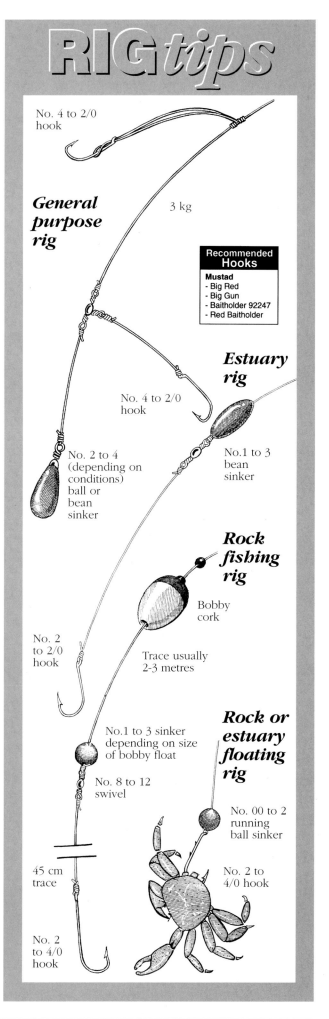

RIGtips

General purpose rig

No. 4 to 2/0 hook

3 kg

No. 4 to 2/0 hook

No. 2 to 4 (depending on conditions) ball or bean sinker

Recommended Hooks
Mustad
- Big Red
- Big Gun
- Baitholder 92247
- Red Baitholder

Estuary rig

No.1 to 3 bean sinker

Rock fishing rig

Bobby cork

Trace usually 2-3 metres

No. 2 to 2/0 hook

No.1 to 3 sinker depending on size of bobby float

No. 8 to 12 swivel

45 cm trace

No. 2 to 4/0 hook

Rock or estuary floating rig

No. 00 to 2 running ball sinker

No. 2 to 4/0 hook

Crickets & Grasshoppers

Crickets are a small burrowing insect related to the grasshopper family. Their daylight burrowing is matched by night time flights that often end with the insect in the water. Surface feeding freshwater fish like trout and bass are very keen on crickets. Bass in particular show a regular preference for crickets, while trout tend to hunt them late in the autumn when the crickets are on the wing.

Tasmanian highland grasshopper.

Most anglers have heard the chirpy cricket sound from its burrow in the grass and while they are relatively common they are hard to find in numbers big enough to make sufficient bait for a mornings fishing.

Despite the low numbers though they are a deadly bait in the right situation.

Where to Find Crickets

Crickets can be found under fallen timber, in brick piles and in grassy areas in small burrows. Some species of cricket are also common in the sandy areas surrounding coastal rivers and streams. Not surprisingly these are known as sand crickets.

Crickets are also strongly attracted to bright lights at night and can be collected at places like tennis courts, sports ovals and other areas with bright signage or lighting. Cricket collecting anglers may appear like leaping lunatics to passing strangers but the effort is often worthwhile.

How to Catch Crickets

During daylight, walking around any paddock or cleared area lifting timber, iron or rocks will reveal a few crickets which can be grabbed and placed in a container.

Spending a few warm summer nights loitering around any well lit area will yield a dozen crickets and grasshoppers too.

The crickets are picked up by hand and dropped into a container full of grass. The container must also have a fitted lid.

Grasshoppers

Grasshoppers are a rich food source for freshwater

How to Use Crickets

Anglers seeking bass usually fish the crickets suspended about 1.2 metres under a small bubble or bobby float. This is then drifted with the current past a likely snag, along a deep bank or allowed to float under overhanging vegetation.

The baits are also fished on the surface at dawn and dusk during the warmer months.

Trout anglers use them in similar fashion. On streams, they are drifted along with a greased leader using either no weight or a small bubble float. During the main part of the day they can be suspended below a float and allowed to drift in mid-water.

On lakes they are mostly fished suspended below a bubble float in mid-water. Again, when the fish are actively cruising the surface, the crickets are fished live and struggling on the surface and cast with the aid of a bubble float.

Surface rigs are no more than a hook and greased line and a bubble float if necessary. Rigs suspending the bait are usually made up of a couple of very small split shot set beneath a bubble float. Hook sizes from No.8 to No.6 are used on trout while No.6 to No.4 are ideal for bass.

How to Use Grasshoppers

Grasshoppers can be fished on the surface if the fish can be seen rising, in mid-water or along the bottom if there is no surface activity. Fishing them on the surface may demand no more than a hook or a hook and a small bubble float.

Grasshopper hooked by the wings for lightweight presentation.

When fishing the bait in mid-water or along the bottom, a small split shot will ensure the struggling grasshopper is swept along where a trout or bass is likely to find it. A small float can also be used in this type of presentation. In the dams or on larger rivers the grasshoppers can be fished on the bottom or suspended under a float.

Hook sizes for grasshoppers are usually No.6 to No.4 on trout while up to 1/0 size are used on bass and yellowbelly. The hoppers are usually hooked through the tough collar area of their thorax, just behind the head. Alternatively, the hook can be threaded through the body from head to tail so the hook protrudes from the abdomen.

Some anglers fishing unweighted surface presentations, where they want a struggling bait, pass the hook through the wings at their base near the body.

fish particularly during high summer when large numbers of these insects are on the wing. At these times trout in particular 'tune-in' to these insects. Native species like yellowbelly, silver perch, bass and even Murray cod will likewise use an abundant supply of grasshoppers to advantage.

Anglers can see the signs fairly readily. If walking through a paddock or driving down a track to the river puts dozens of grasshoppers on the wing, then the same thing will be happening along the stream, river or lake and some of the hoppers will end up in the water.

With the hoppers landing in the water on a regular basis, the fish can't help but find them. Small to medium sized trout streams tend to fish best when grasshoppers are on the menu.

Where to Find Grasshoppers

The presence of grasshoppers is fairly obvious to anyone walking or driving through a paddock. They usually lift into the air with a distinct clatter of wings and are very easily seen once disturbed.

Grasshoppers tend to prefer paddock areas with medium height grass. Areas of short grass offer them little protection from predators.

How to Catch Grasshoppers

Grasshoppers are cold blooded animals and need the heat of the day to warm them up and get them functioning.

The best time to catch them is very early in the morning before they become fully active. At this time instead of fluttering away and out of reach the insect can only hop or flutter a metre or so and is easily caught in a fine gauge net.

Grasshoppers are also attracted to any bright lights at night and can be easily netted or grabbed by hand.

The range of species and the size of hoppers varies from area to area, but in general it is the large common grasshopper that is keenly sought as bait.

Handling

Like most insect baits, crickets and grasshoppers will keep very well in a fridge with a cool but not cold temperature setting. Store the collected baits in a container half filled with long grass. The insects will keep for a month or more stored this way.

Don't be lulled by their lethargy when removed from the fridge. As soon as they start to warm they will fly so keep them in a lidded container and be careful! when reaching for each bait.

Alternatively, use a polystyrene vegetable box with a mixture of sand, soil and grass clippings. This needs plenty of small ventilation holes in the sides or lid. They will live about two to three weeks stored in this way. Place the container in a cool, shady spot.

Points of Note

When collecting crickets from under bits of timber, iron and rocks in paddocks and scrubby areas be prepared for more than just crickets. The same habitats are frequented by snakes and a range of spiders. Always look carefully at what is under the timber or iron before pouncing on the fleeing crickets.

Fish feeding on the surface for grasshoppers are usually very active and easily seen. When they are actively seeking surface hoppers they will often feed on little else so the angler has no choice but to use grasshoppers or go without a bite.

Carrying a fine gauge net in the car helps if a few insects have to be caught quickly. Alternatively, carry some gauze that can be quickly fitted inside a landing net and send someone off to snare a few grasshoppers or crickets.

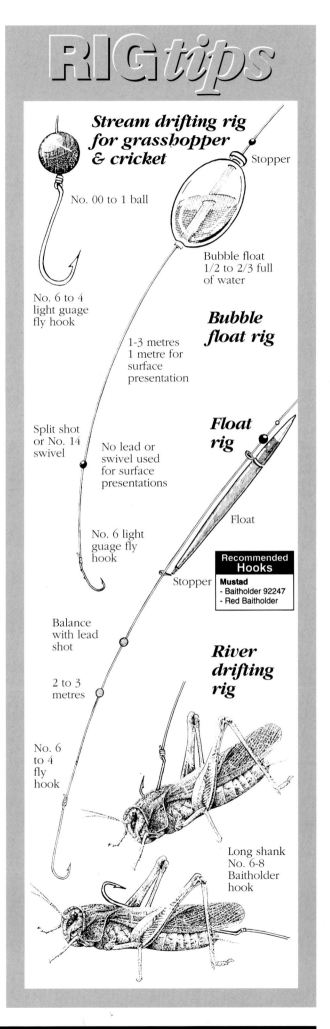

RIGtips

Stream drifting rig for grasshopper & cricket

No. 00 to 1 ball

No. 6 to 4 light guage fly hook

Stopper

Bubble float 1/2 to 2/3 full of water

Bubble float rig

1-3 metres 1 metre for surface presentation

Split shot or No. 14 swivel

No lead or swivel used for surface presentations

Float rig

Float

No. 6 light guage fly hook

Stopper

Recommended Hooks
Mustad
- Baitholder 92247
- Red Baitholder

Balance with lead shot

River drifting rig

2 to 3 metres

No. 6 to 4 fly hook

Long shank No. 6-8 Baitholder hook

Cunjevoi

Above: Profile of cunje.
Below: Cunjevoi can be found in clusters on ocean rocks. Take care when harvesting.

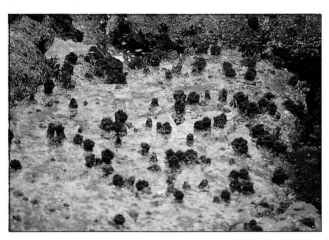

Cunjevoi (*Pyura stolonifera*) or cunje as it is called is a type of sea squirt and regardless of its appearance is actually an animal and not a plant as many people think.

It is roughly cylindrical in shape and grows approximately 15 cm high and 5 cm in diameter. The cunje has a large leathery casing dark red to black in colour with the rich, juicy bait protected within.

Cunje is regarded as one of the best, all-round rock fishing baits with most of the forage type fish being interested in taking it. Fish like bream, luderick, drummer, rock blackfish, sweep, leatherjackets, wrasse, groper and many others all feed aggressively on cunje.

Where to Find It

Cunje is found on ocean rocks and in areas close to the sea inside deep estuaries and harbours from southern Queensland, New South Wales, Victoria and South Australia.

It is most prevalent in the sub-littoral zone with moderate to strong wave action. It can grow singularly or in clumps and often covers entire rock shelves.

How to Collect It

Cunje is usually collected at low tide when the larger growths are exposed and easy to reach.

As with any pursuit on the ocean rocks care must be taken to watch the sea while bait collecting on lower, exposed edges. Don't try cutting cunje for bait if the area is being washed by surf. Wait until the tide is low or the conditions are calm before collecting the bait.

Cunje is cut from the rocks with a sharp, heavy-bladed knife. In New South Wales the usual practice was to use a mattock if a large amount of cunje was to be harvested, this is now prohibited and there is a limit of 20 cunje in possession per person. This is usually enough for bait in most situations.

Handling

The large, sharp knife is also used to extract the cunje from its leathery casing. This is done by carefully cutting downwards using the point of the knife around the water squirt or nipple looking area on top of the cunje.

Once this area is free, the side of the casing can be cut open wide enough to allow

How to Use It

The firm parts of the cunje are used to secure the hook. By leaving the water squirt nipple in place the hook can also be put through this for extra holding power. Most large cunje provide two to four baits depending on the size of the bait being used. The soft fleshy part of the bait is always left on as it attracts the fish and does not seem to hamper the take despite its apparent bulk.

Hook size usually dictates bait size but don't be scared to use a large bait as the rock dwelling fish know how to handle cunje. Hook sizes should match the fish being sought, though No.2 to 3/0 would cover most species. Small rounded hook types like the Suicide pattern are ideal for fishing with cunje.

The important point is to ensure the hook is located in the firm parts of the bait to allow for good casting and to help the bait stay on the hook while it is eaten by the fish.

Top: Cunje casing and bait.
Left: Cunje rigged for use.

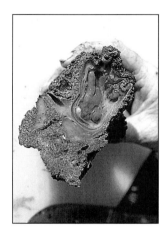

Profile of cunjevoi within its leathery shell.

the index and middle fingers to go down the inside of the casing and extract the bait which is a firm, pulpy flesh.

Once extracted the flesh is stored in a bucket or hip mounted bait carrier or used

as needed while fishing.

Points of Note

Cunje is one of the few baits that is just as appealing to the fish when preserved as it is when fresh. Cunje is also easy to preserve.

To do this, remove it from the casing and allow it to drain on a large amount of newspaper in the fridge for an hour or so.

Mix equal parts of sugar and salt. Place all the cunje in a shallow tray and mix thoroughly with the sugar and salt. Place the thoroughly coated cunje in a large jar and when nearly full top up with more sugar and salt mixture. Seal the jar and place in the bottom of the fridge. The bait will keep for at least 3 months and will be available any time you want to go fishing.

A fine blue groper taken on cunje.

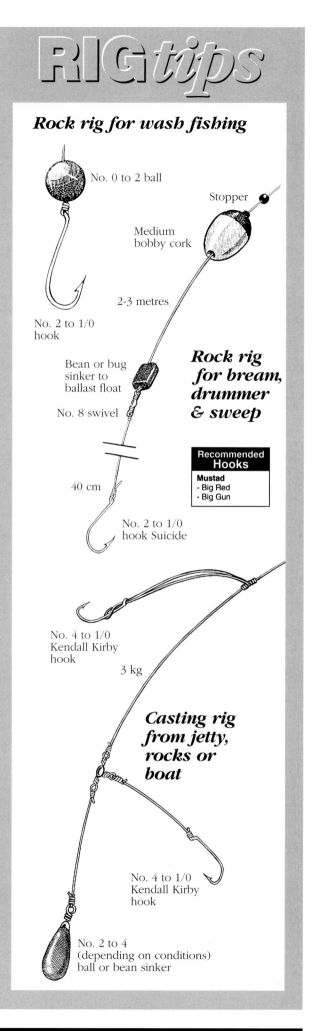

Cut*baits*

Using cut fish baits is a basic saltwater fishing skill. Just about any fish can be used for a cut bait. However, the soft, oily fleshed species are generally the favoured prey of most fish, so using one of those for cut baits makes good sense.

Fish like small tuna, slimy mackerel, yellowtail, mullet, herring, tailor and bonito are among the best cut bait candidates.

How to Prepare It

The secret of using fish baits is in how they are cut and presented. The first rule is to give the fish something it likes to eat in a size and shape that it can easily swallow. Fresh bait is particularly important. If the flesh is soft and flaky it will not hold on the hook very well. If there is a strong current or small pickers about, they will remove the soft flesh leaving just the skin on the hook. Bait which is not fresh is not very appealing to the fish either, but a slice of fresh, firm fish bait with blood and oil still seeping from it will be most appealing.

Cutting a whole fish for bait can be done in a number of ways depending on the size of the bait fish and the type of bait needed for the sort of fishing being done.

The simplest and most useful way of cutting most larger bait fish is to fillet them and then slice the fillets into useable size strips. Always fillet from head to tail as this is the same direction as the muscle structure in the fish.

Most fillets are then cut into long strips which are further cut into pieces that suit both the hook size and the fish being sought. Keep the strips fairly thin by trimming excess meat away.

This is particularly important with striped tuna or big bonito.

When bottom fishing for fish such as bream, snapper and flathead or drifting offshore, the usual strip bait ends up about the size of the index finger. Bigger baits can be used depending on the class of fish being targeted and the size of hook needed to handle them. For mulloway, cod, kingfish, large snapper and others, a large fillet about 15 cm x 6 cm makes a handy bait.

One method of cutting baits used by offshore anglers is to slice a whole bonito, frigate mackerel or other small tuna into pieces while it is still attached to the frame of the fish. Once all the necessary cuts are made a sharp knife simply fillets that side and all the pre-cut baits fall off the fish. This technique is mostly used in hot bite situations where the fish are feeding furiously, and it is important to minimise bait preparation time.

Yellowtail with fillet removed and cut into strips.

How to Use It

Most strip baits are placed on the hook by pushing the point through the flesh and out through the skin. This is done at the thick end of the bait close to the edge of the skin.

The hook is passed through the bait once only. This gives it a very natural presentation in the water and allows the bait to flutter in an enticing fashion. This long, slim bait is also easy for the fish to swallow and leaves the point of the hook in a prime position for the strike.

Many anglers thread the bait onto the hook by passing the point of the hook through the bait several times. This may look satisfactory at the start, but after casting and water pressure from reeling it in, the bait often ends up as an unappealing blob at the end of the hook. The hook point may become covered and miss any fish that does take the bait.

The best solution if the bait needs a little more holding power on the hook is to use two linked hooks. By ganging the hooks in a similar fashion to a tailor rig the bait still looks good but has the added strike power of two points. The bait will also cast very well on this rig.

Another alternative is to pass the hook through the flesh and out through the skin bringing the whole hook through the bait. The point of the hook is then passed back through the bait exactly one hook length from the top exit mark. A half hitch is tied around the top of the bait and the hook eye to hold them together.

Strip baits can be rigged with single or double hooks depending on fish being sought.

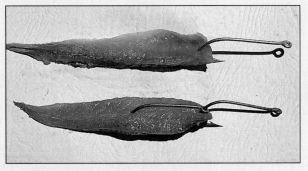

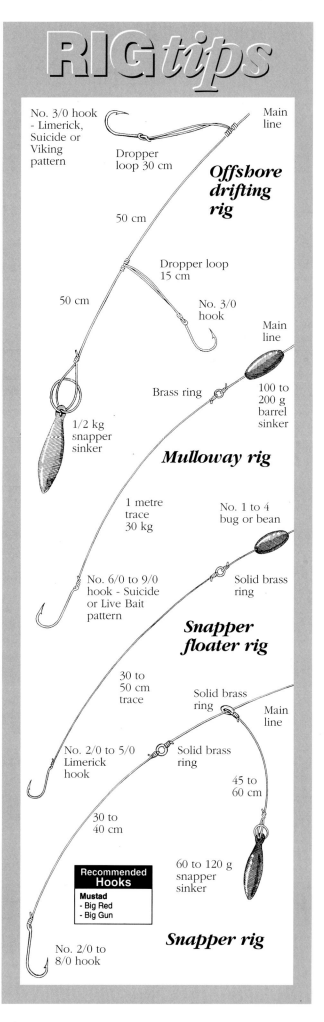

Strip baits are ideal for coral trout and other reef fish.

Points of Note

Cut or strip baits work best when they look natural to the fish. An easy to swallow strip of well presented fresh bait will appeal to many species.

A sharp knife is a vital part of the system, making filleting and slicing easy,

providing exactly the right shape and size baits required. A blunt knife will rip and mash baits causing more problems than it is worth.

When working with strip baits attention to detail is most important. Sharp knives and well presented baits add up to more fish.

Strip baits can be secured to the hook using a half hitch.

Cuttlefish

uttlefish are another of the *Cephalopoda* family related to the squid and octopus and a handy bait for a range of offshore fish species.

The cuttlefish is actually an aggressive hunter of small fish, prawns and crabs. It glides slowly around the ocean floor searching for prey. When it spots a likely target it stalks it until it is within range of its hugely

Strip baits of cuttlefish are always a good stand-by on snapper.

elastic strike tentacles. These shoot out at lighting speed to grab the unwary prey.

Like the squid and octopus cuttlefish are sold as both bait and food for humans, although they are much tougher than squid which keeps their price down.

The fish don't seem to notice the difference and the species that like to eat squid also like cuttlefish. Fish like yellowtail kingfish, cobia, mulloway, snapper, samson fish, morwong, cod and other reef dwellers will all take cuttlefish readily.

Where to Find Them

Cuttlefish are commonly found in deep estuaries, harbours and bays as well as being very common offshore and along the ocean rocks. Juvenile cuttlefish tend to hang together in groups particularly around well established seagrass beds and rocky reefs.

They range in size from about 15 cm to over a metre and 20 kg in weight. The common cuttlefish used as bait is about as big as a fist and is mostly caught commercially by prawn trawlers.

Offshore the very large cuttlefish are regularly encountered by anglers as many tend to inhabit reef

areas or occur along ocean rocks and kelp beds.

How to Catch Them

Cuttlefish are mostly purchased for bait as catching them is mostly an incidental capture that cannot be relied on for a regular bait supply.

The common trawled cuttlefish is also very inexpensive and so it is rarely worthwhile to try to catch these animals for bait.

The big oceanic cuttlefish usually hook themselves on gear set for something else. This is particularly true in the case of pilchards rigged on ganged hooks, but they hook up on almost anything.

Sometimes they intercept a struggling fish on the line as it is being played to the surface and hang on grimly until lead to a waiting net.

Once captured, the cuttlefish will spray the captors, the boat or anything else in the vicinity with liberal quantities of thick black ink. When this starts to happen some people question the work involved in landing them just for a little extra bait.

How to Use Them

Cuttlefish are mostly cut and used in strip form for most angling situations. The head is removed and may be used whole or in sections.

The body section is opened and layed flat with a knife and then cut into strips about as big as an index finger. The gut and distinctive cuttlebone is discarded.

These strips are then hooked once only at one end and used as bait. There is no need to try and thread the bait onto the hook.

Most cuttlefish are used offshore and hooks from 3/0 to 6/0 are the most popular depending on the species being sought. Hooks like the Limerick, Tarpon and Live Bait patterns which have no set or kirb are preferred for fishing with the strip type baits provided by the cuttlefish.

Cuttlefish plus rigged baits.

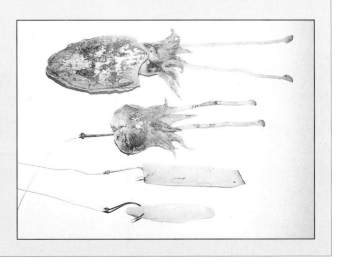

Handling

Most of the small cuttlefish are purchased and used on a trip by trip basis. However they do freeze very well and they only need to be thoroughly washed, placed in plastic bags and frozen if wanted for future trips.

The larger cuttlefish that do get caught can be a bit of a challenge for most anglers. The tentacles are removed easily and make good strip baits. The body meat is thick and useful but it takes a lot of mess and mucking around to get at it.

Many anglers go through this process once and don't worry about it again. All the work is hardly worth it for the amount of bait yielded. On the opposite side, once a few of these big cuttlefish have been handled, the angler quickly learns how to remove the bait with a minimum of fuss and mess.

The freshly removed flesh and tentacles is washed and packed ready for freezing.

Points of Note

Not only is the cuttlefish unusual for the unique internal shell, the cuttlebone, it possesses but the ink which the cuttlefish uses as a means of defence, was for many years used as a sepia pigment. Although it is very stable, it does tend to fade with the passage of time.

Cuttlefish can get to very large sizes like this 13 kg model.

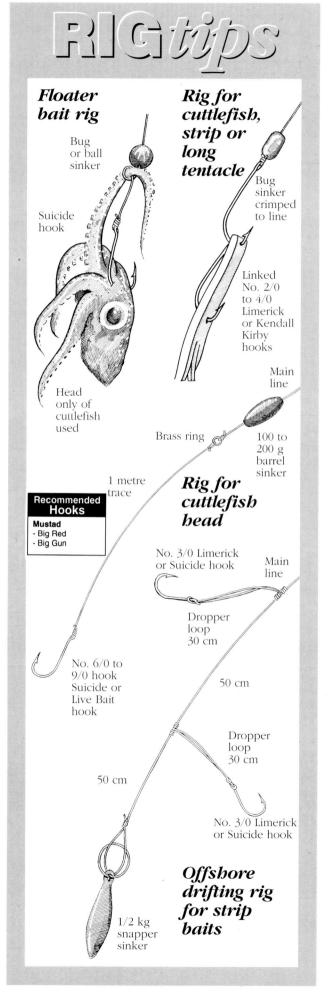

Floater bait rig

Bug or ball sinker

Suicide hook

Head only of cuttlefish used

1 metre trace

Recommended Hooks
Mustad
- Big Red
- Big Gun

No. 6/0 to 9/0 hook Suicide or Live Bait hook

50 cm

1/2 kg snapper sinker

Rig for cuttlefish, strip or long tentacle

Bug sinker crimped to line

Linked No. 2/0 to 4/0 Limerick or Kendall Kirby hooks

Main line

Brass ring

100 to 200 g barrel sinker

Rig for cuttlefish head

No. 3/0 Limerick or Suicide hook

Main line

Dropper loop 30 cm

50 cm

Dropper loop 30 cm

No. 3/0 Limerick or Suicide hook

Offshore drifting rig for strip baits

Bread, like a few other popular baits, is something simple, man-made, and opportunistic fish like to eat it. In some areas, the fish get 'tuned-in' to bread and it becomes the only bait they will take.

Mullet near picnic areas tend to fall into this category. Lots of other fish like bread, with bream, rock blackfish, luderick, sweep, garfish, slimy mackerel, yellowtail, tommy ruff, trevally, herring and carp all being regular takers.

Apart from its use as bait, bread is an essential berley for many fish. All of the above species are attracted by bread berley as are many others. Bread is an essential fishing bait and berley.

Bread as Bait – How to Use It

Using bread can be an exact science in certain locations. The best breads for bait are usually those straight from the baker. The centre or white part of the fresh loaf is soft and doughy making it easy to form into a tight, little ball or teardrop that will stay on the hook.

Bread that is dry or stale is not suitable as it will be brittle when put on a hook or comes in contact with the water. If it must be used, it needs some water added and be kneaded (worked with the hands) to get the firm consistencies needed to stay on a hook.

Prepared bread baits and rigs.

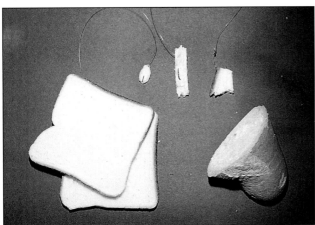

Occasionally fish become extremely educated and fussy about how they want the bread before they will take it. This usually means presenting the bait in a soft, wet form, not tight and doughy. When using bread in this manner the angler only gets one shot at the fish as the bait comes away from the hook very easily. It is usually a tussle of wits in this form of angling and the target is usually mullet or garfish.

The crust part of the bread is vital as fishing bait. Being naturally tougher than the white or centre part of the bread it stays on a hook much better and can sustain more bite impact when wet than the rest of the loaf.

Bread crusts are the best part to use when looking for larger fish like bream, rock blackfish and carp. Again the fresh loaf is best as the crust is toughest at this time.

It is usually used in strips and threaded onto the hook much like a worm. Sliced bread makes using strips easy, as the slice width is about perfect for use as bait. Just tear the crust length to suit the size of the hook and thread it on.

On smaller mouthed fish like mullet, garfish, sweep and luderick, sliced crust is still the best bait but it is usually torn or cut into 1 cm segments to suit the small hooks used. When used like this, the hook is passed once through the bait.

Bread as Berley – How to Use It

Bread berley is made by mulching bread and mixing in some water to make a pulpy mixture that can be thrown or directed into the fishing area. It is usually important that the bread berley sink and not float away, taking the fish with it.

To ensure this happens, the pulp is squeezed firmly to remove any air bubbles before tossing it into the water.

There are other tricks to help the bread to sink. Many anglers mix the pulped wet bread with sand. Some use berley cages and berley floats or other devices to deliver the berley to their fishing area.

While bread alone is a good berley it can be improved by adding a few mulched pilchards or tuna oil to the mixture to give it a little aroma and more attraction to the fish.

Points of Note

The best bread for fishing is usually white, sliced bread. If only the doughy centre is needed a whole loaf is fine. While other types of bread work, the white bread seems to attract the fish and it holds together better than wholemeal or breads full of seeds and what not. The key to success though is to use a fresh loaf.

Dough

Dough is a mixture of flour and water which is blended to form a consistent material that will stay on a hook.

Like bread, dough has considerable appeal to opportunistic feeders or to fish that have learned to find food in association with man. Places like picnic areas, around wharves and at outlets where some sort of

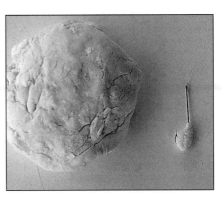

A lump of dough and a baited hook ready for use.

food is contained in the discharged waste water.

How to Make Dough

Apart from the obvious pun, dough is made by mixing flour and water. The combination of the two starts with a flour base of one or two cups and water is added bit by bit to get the mixture to the right consistency.

When the mixture starts to 'firm' do not add any more water. Rather continue to stir the mixture and add flour by sprinkling it finely over the top of the now forming dough.

It should be possible to work the now formed dough by hand without it sticking to the hands. This is the test of whether the consistency is right.

Form the dough into a fist-sized ball and coat lightly with dry flour.

The end result is much the same as what a baker does with bread dough before it goes into the oven.

How to Use Dough

The dough should be pliable and easy to work but 'dry' so it does not stick to the hands. To use on the fish it is rolled into a teardrop or ball shape and put on the hook. A good dough will stay firmly on the hook without any problems.

Pudding

Pudding is the name used to describe a mixture of flour, meat, cheese and bread in varying proportions.

Various blends of pud-

& pudding

ding have been made famous by bream anglers over the years. These often aromatic mixtures seem to attract bream readily while other, unwanted species like catfish and eels leave the pudding alone.

The great attraction of pudding is that the bait can be made in the kitchen and then used to go fishing.

How to Make Pudding

The main ingredients in most puddings includes bread, dough, cheese, garlic sausage and tinned sardines. The aim is to produce a fish attracting bait in a form that will stay on the hook.

To make a pudding, remove about half a cup of bread from a fresh loaf of bread. Add similar quantities of cheddar cheese and finely chopped garlic sausage. The mixture is worked together by hand until combined.

The bread and cheese base can also be combined with tinned sardines or anchovies. This is pulped together to make a very attractive pudding.

Another variation on this recipe is finely chopped mussels or oysters combined with the doughy contents of a packet of pastry.

These mixtures can also be added to with a little strong smelling fish oil.

How to Use Pudding

The key to both dough and pudding mixtures is to produce a bait that will stay on the hook readily, which it does if mixed correctly.

The bait is usually formed into a teardrop shape and the hook placed through it. Alternatively, many anglers use the hook as a centre and press or roll the bait onto the hook.

Either way, the hook ends up in the centre of the bait ready for whatever takes the pudding.

Hook sizes should be chosen to suit the fish being sought. On mullet, gar, ruff and other small fish, hooks from No.10 to No.6 are about right. On bream and similar sized fish No.3 to 1/0 is appropriate.

Points of Note

Dough is often an essential part of the pier fishing scene and using it well takes a bit of practice but it does catch fish.

The essential secret of both dough and pudding is to get the consistency right so it all stays on the hook.

Pudding baits are mostly aimed at bream fishing in quiet estuary waters, it will not stay on the hook in ocean type fishing and it should be cast gently rather than force cast.

The ingredients of a good pudding can include bread, cheese, garlic sausage and sardines. It is usually formed into a teardrop shape and placed onto the hook.

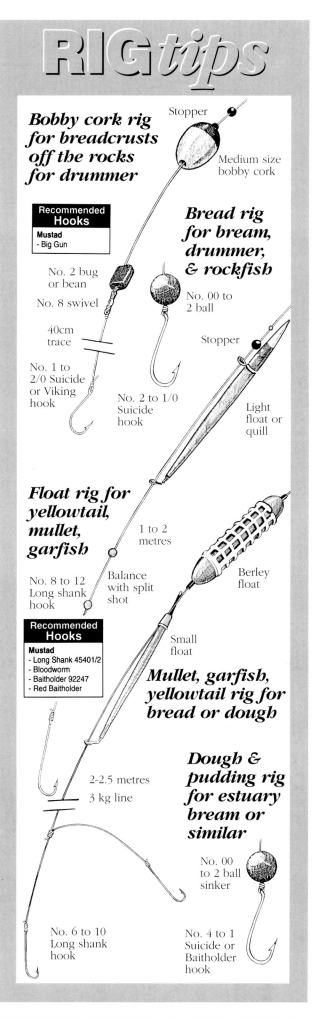

Bobby cork rig for breadcrusts off the rocks for drummer

Stopper

Medium size bobby cork

Recommended Hooks

Mustad
- Big Gun

No. 2 bug or bean

No. 8 swivel

40cm trace

No. 1 to 2/0 Suicide or Viking hook

Bread rig for bream, drummer, & rockfish

No. 00 to 2 ball

Stopper

No. 2 to 1/0 Suicide hook

Light float or quill

Float rig for yellowtail, mullet, garfish

1 to 2 metres

No. 8 to 12 Long shank hook

Balance with split shot

Berley float

Small float

Recommended Hooks

Mustad
- Long Shank 45401/2
- Bloodworm
- Baitholder 92247
- Red Baitholder

Mullet, garfish, yellowtail rig for bread or dough

Dough & pudding rig for estuary bream or similar

2-2.5 metres

3 kg line

No. 00 to 2 ball sinker

No. 6 to 10 Long shank hook

No. 4 to 1 Suicide or Baitholder hook

Gar*fish*

Garfish are a common estuary and ocean species found right around the country. They are an important bait fish and a quality food fish and are keenly sought by recreational anglers and commercial fishermen.

Garfish spend most of their time feeding at or near the surface and they are easily seen by observant anglers as they cruise about in a particular area.

Various species of garfish are used as bait and some do make better baits than others. In temperate areas, the sea garfish is much better bait than the river garfish.

The two species are easily distinguished with sea garfish losing almost all of their scales on capture while those of the river garfish stay firmly in place.

In northern areas, the thick set snubnosed gar is popular along with a close relative of the sea garfish which is found along protected coastal beaches.

Because garfish are popular as both food and bait, they are readily available through bait shops and seafood merchants. They are often sold fresh in premium condition or packaged and frozen as bait.

Garfish sold as bait are often packaged according to size. Small garfish are very popular with tailor and salmon anglers, while anglers seeking larger targets like mackerel, kingfish or marlin prefer larger sized garfish that can be rigged to swim naturally.

Where to Find Them

Garfish feed around estuary weed beds, oyster leases, on the edges of current lines and often around jetties.

They are attracted to jetties for the food and shelter they provide and in particular any area that is brightly lit at night.

Sea garfish are also very common around ocean rocks where they congregate in sheltered areas around islands, in coves and over kelp beds.

Sea garfish are regularly caught on bait grounds used by offshore anglers using berley to attract other small bait fish.

The tropical species are more common on the tide lines and areas where the current forms an eddy. They also school along sheltered beaches and near the mouth of creeks and rivers where they join the ocean. The tropical garfish varieties are hard to catch on rod and reel as they have a diet of very small planktonic creatures and tend not to bite very often on baited hooks.

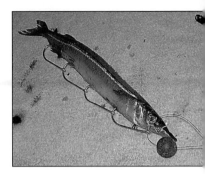

Garfish rigged as a troll bait on ganged hooks for Spanish mackerel.

How to Catch Them

Apart from being good bait, catching garfish can be absorbing angling. Many anglers chase garfish for both sport and food rather than for bait. Their habit of leaping when hooked, a plucky fight plus being a good table fish makes them a popular angling target despite their small size.

How to Use Them

There are lots of fish in the sea that like to eat garfish. Anglers use them as strip baits, whole on gangs, whole rigged to skip or swim or live if the situation allows. How the bait is used depends on what the angler is trying to catch.

The shiny fillet of a sea garfish is extremely tempting to opportunistic feeders like bream, snapper, trevally, tailor and flathead. The fillet is sliced off the gar with a sharp knife and then cut to the desired length or strip.

The bait is best presented by passing the hook once only through the bait near to one end so it looks and moves naturally through the water. Some anglers use two linked hooks to help present the strip bait naturally but also increase the hook-up rate on fish like flathead and tailor.

The four linked hook gang is a classic and deadly effective method of catching tailor, salmon, Spanish mackerel and other predatory fish. The gangs are usually made using 4/0 or 5/0 Limericks or tinned Kendall Kirby types. For small pencil gars, 3/0 gangs are very useful.

The ganged hook rig is baited so that the head of the bait faces the angler and the hook closest to the angler goes through the eye of the bait. Measuring the hooks against the bait is important so the gar is presented in a natural and life-like manner.

Rigged garfish are used by anglers trolling for mackerel, kingfish, tuna, tailor, marlin, sailfish and other predators. Mackerel and tailor trollers use four hook gangs often made up on Tarpon type hooks for extra strength. A lead head jig or other lead moulding is used as a keel to help make the bait swim straight and not spin as it is trolled along.

Live baiting with garfish requires fine gauge hooks so the garfish is not badly injured. Smaller sized hooks than used for most live bait are recommended. Most garfish used as live bait are hooked under the bottom jaw or down near the tail or above or below the lateral line.

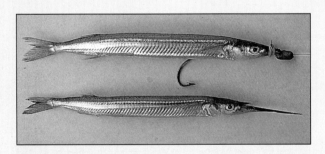

Above: Garfish rigged for trolling.
Below: Garfish rigged on ganged hooks are used by anglers seeking tailor and salmon.

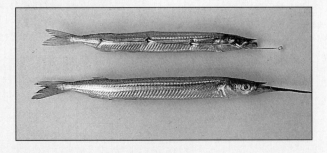

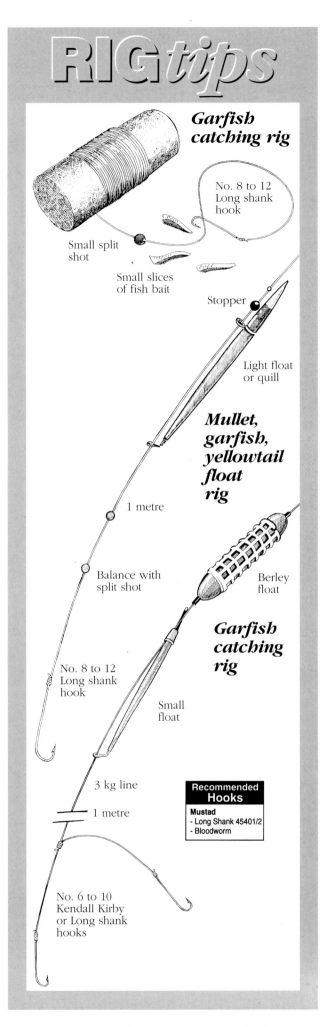

Garfish catching rig

No. 8 to 12
Long shank
hook

Small split
shot

Small slices
of fish bait

Stopper

Light float
or quill

Mullet, garfish, yellowtail float rig

1 metre

Balance with
split shot

Berley
float

No. 8 to 12
Long shank
hook

Small
float

Garfish catching rig

3 kg line

1 metre

No. 6 to 10
Kendall Kirby
or Long shank
hooks

Recommended Hooks
Mustad
- Long Shank 45401/2
- Bloodworm

Spanish mackerel are fierce predators on garfish.

Garfish are caught using very small hooks, usually No.8 to No.12 Long Shanks and light lines of 1 to 3 kg. Boat anglers on ocean bait grounds can use a light handline with just a small hook on the end and no lead to catch garfish from the berley trail.

Anglers looking deliberately for garfish prefer a long whippy rod similar to those used for luderick. This type of rod handles the float rigs used to catch garfish well and suits this style of fishing best.

Either single or two hook rigs are used often with no sinker and about 20 to 40 cm of line between the hook and the float. Best baits are pinches of prawn, small strips of fish (often garfish), bread and maggots.

Berley is an essential ingredient when seeking gar-fish. It brings them to the fishing location, encourages them to bite carelessly and keeps them biting in the area. Berley made up of finely mulched wet bread, wet bread crumbs or rolled dry biscuits all work well.

Because the fish feed at or near the surface much of the angling is visual and the fish can often be seen taking the bait. Wait until the bait disappears into the fish's mouth before striking.

Tropical anglers catch most of their garfish in cast nets or bait nets. Cast nets are used on visible schools of fish while bait nets are used to haul shallow corners and other likely areas.

Garfish are quick and often out-speed cast nets but hauled bait nets are highly productive, particularly if the fish are schooling in a restricted area.

Gar*fish*

How to Rig Garfish

Game fish rigs can be as simple or as complicated as the angler cares to make them.

The simplest and amongst the best rig available is the one illustrated here using .022 gauge brown single strand wire.

The hook used is a needle eye or round eye Tarpon type and a tag end of wire about 1.5 cm long left after the traditional barrel roll and haywire twist has been tied. The tag end is aligned so that it sits straight up in the opposite direction to the hook pointing straight down.

The method of baiting is shown with the garfish being secured to the wire tag with a small elastic band. So long as everything is straight the garfish will troll at speeds up to 6 knots.

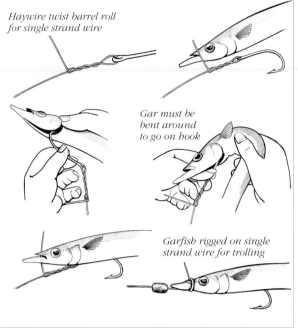

Haywire twist barrel roll for single strand wire

Gar must be bent around to go on hook

Garfish rigged on single strand wire for trolling

Handling

Garfish tend to be highly strung and don't survive very well in most bait tanks. They will live in large bait tanks but not always for long periods.

As a rule, most garfish are caught for later bait use and keeping them alive is not generally a major issue.

As with most bait fish, the best way to keep garfish in top condition after capture is to drop them into a cooler filled with a half ice, half seawater mixture. This kills them quickly and maintains them in ideal condition until use or preparation for the freezer.

Points of Note

With most rigs using whole

Gut*baits*

Both chicken gut and mullet gut are sold as fishing bait and their primary target is bream, a fish which seems to be willing to eat just about anything that closely resembles food. Other fish are regularly caught using gut baits, including flathead, trevally, school mulloway and reef fish. Having said that, there are times and places when chicken and mullet gut will out fish any other bait. Some of this knowledge is often gained through local bait shops or by talking to anglers working the area.

Some areas where gut type baits are likely to work include outlet or wash-down drains from Fish Co-operatives, around fish cleaning tables which bream haunt under the cover of darkness and similar locations.

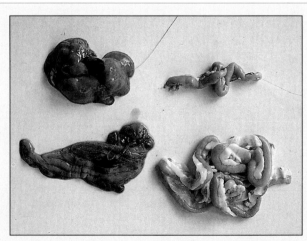

Mullet gut and chicken gut set on hook.

How to Use Chicken Gut

The bait is tough and stays on the hook well. It's white or light colour makes it easy for fish to see, although the bait works well at night and in discoloured water, so it must have an attractive smell to the fish.

Chicken gut is put on the hook much like a worm with segments being looped on until the desired size bait is achieved. Best hook sizes are usually No.2 to 2/0 with Suicide patterns the best choice.

How to Use Mullet Gut

Each individual mullet gut makes one bait, with the hook placed through the hard ball part of the gut known as the 'onion'. This hard section keeps the gut firmly on the hook. The rest of the bait is soft tissue and while attractive to the fish, it will not hold a hook easily. The gut is bulky but soft and the bream have little trouble eating it. While it is not a pleasant bait to use, mullet gut does catch fish and in places is both popular and successful.

Hooks are the same as for chicken gut and the best rig is just a small ball sinker sitting right on the hook.

Garfish rigged as a troll bait on a single hook and heavy monofilament leader for billfish and tuna.

garfish the bill is broken off or cut off with pliers to stop the bait twisting from water pressure against the bill.

Some anglers use soft fuse wire to wrap the beak to the top hook to stop the bait spinning and to secure it to the hooks. This helps secure the bait and can make for the quick rigging of the bait.

Large bream are often caught using chicken or mullet gut.

Gut baits also work in general fishing situations including offshore and around the rocks. Offshore, snapper will definitely take chicken gut while both baits work around the rocks on species such as bream, trevally and sweep.

Chicken Gut

Chicken gut is processed and autoclaved prior to its packaging for bait. It is fairly clean and easy to handle and does not have an offensive smell, unless left in the sun for an hour or two.

Mullet Gut

Mullet gut is a smelly, slimy and offensive bait under most conditions. Although it does catch a lot of fish at times it is not a pleasant bait to use.

Points of Note

All gut baits should be kept on ice during use to ensure they don't spoil which can happen quickly in hot weather.

It is also important to remember that gut baits have a very high bacterial level and care should be taken to wash and wipe the hands when the bait is being used. This is particularly important when tying knots or handling food.

Getting a severe stomach upset from the bait is possible when using these baits if care and attention to detail is not maintained.

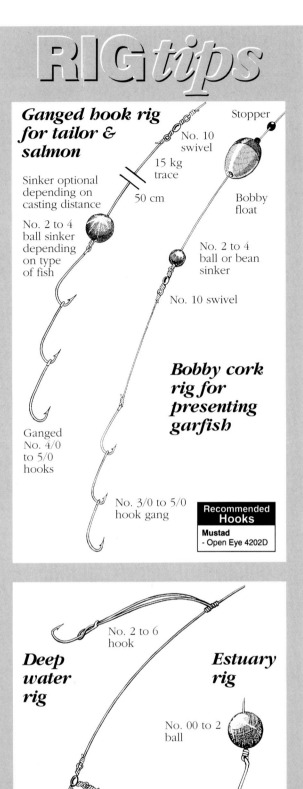

Ganged hook rig for tailor & salmon

Sinker optional depending on casting distance

No. 2 to 4 ball sinker depending on type of fish

Ganged No. 4/0 to 5/0 hooks

No. 3/0 to 5/0 hook gang

Stopper

No. 10 swivel

15 kg trace

50 cm

Bobby float

No. 2 to 4 ball or bean sinker

No. 10 swivel

Bobby cork rig for presenting garfish

Recommended **Hooks**
Mustad
- Open Eye 4202D

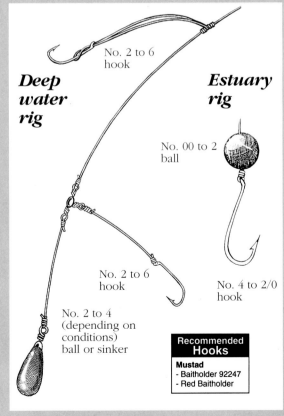

Deep water rig

No. 2 to 6 hook

No. 2 to 6 hook

No. 2 to 4 (depending on conditions) ball or sinker

Estuary rig

No. 00 to 2 ball

No. 4 to 2/0 hook

Recommended **Hooks**
Mustad
- Baitholder 92247
- Red Baitholder

Hardy*heads*

Hardyheads swimming in live bait tank.

Hardyheads *(Pranesus ogilbyi)* are a robust little bait fish that can be bought or caught and makes good bait both dead and alive.

They are commonly 60 to 100 mm long and silvery white in colour with a distinctive silver stripe along the side and a layer of firm scales.

They are often overshadowed by the more popular whitebait and frogmouthed pilchards from the freezer cabinet, but they are a worthwhile bait none the less.

Hardyheads are mostly used as an estuary bait but they will work effectively on offshore fish and are regularly used as both bait and berley on inshore tuna like northern bluefin.

Where to Find Them

Hardyheads will congregate around wharves and jetties and along the edges of sandbanks, weed beds and channels. They are a school fish and are often found in very large numbers.

Hardyheads are also very common over weed beds in quite bays and are often located in small numbers sleeping on the surface in the shallows at night by prawners.

Hardyheads are a distinctly shaped fish and can be easily spotted swimming about, particularly if wearing polaroid glasses. Knowing hardyheads are in the fishing area makes catching them by hook or net much easier.

How to Catch Them

Around wharves and jetties and from boats, hardyheads can be caught on small baited hooks and very light lines. A 2 or 3 kg line rigged with a No.10 Long Shank hook and a very small split shot pinched onto the line about 20 cm from the hook is perfect.

The hardyheads are berleyed with finely mulched wet bread and the hook is baited with a pinch of prawn or a small slice of fish. These baits are fished near the berley and once the hardyheads start biting, they can be caught quite quickly.

In Queensland they are readily caught in both cast nets and hauled bait nets. This type of bait catching

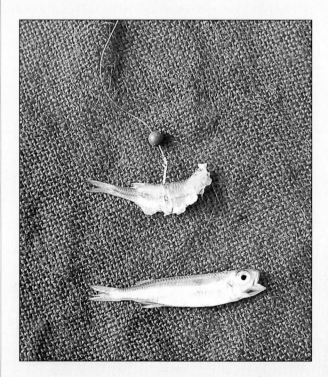

Above: Hardyhead profile.
Right: Hooking a hardyhead for use as live bait.

How to Use Them

Hardyheads are very good live bait for flathead, school mulloway, mangrove jack, trevally, cod and big bream.

Like nearly all small fish baits they work better when alive than when dead.

Fished live, they can be hooked through the bottom jaw and out through the roof of the mouth or through the back in the first dorsal fin area. The head hooking system is used when drifting or in fast current and the dorsal rig is used when anchored or for fishing a specific location or using some form of float.

If being fished as dead bait, two linked 2/0 Limericks will ensure good presentation and a high hook-up rate. Alternatively, a single hook placed through the head from the underside out through the top will work very well. Hooks suited to this style of presentation include Suicide, Tarpon, Live Bait, Kendall Kirby and Viking.

Above: Using a bait net is the most effective way to catch hardyheads.
Below: Large catch of haryheads used for bait and berley for tuna in Morton Bay.

equipment allows for a large number of hardyheads to be captured.

As stated earlier, prawners working with bright lights and dip nets catch a lot of hardyheads at night and this method is an easy way of collecting a few live baits for the following day.

Handling

Hardyheads handle very well and will survive for long periods in a bait tank or container filled with seawater and an aerator.

They also freeze very well and can simply be bagged and frozen if required for later use.

Points of Note

Spotting hardyheads either from a jetty or shore can sometimes be difficult. From a jetty the thing to look for is a ghost-like fish shape that drifts around in the fishing area, rising and falling in and out of vision as it pulses about.

Often, once one of these fish are spotted, many more can be seen by looking deeper into the water.

Schools can often be observed moving or feeding in shallow water by locating their shadows on the bottom sand. Again once spotted, a quite large school can be seen in an area that at first appearance seemed to hold few if any fish.

This little trick applies to lots of small bait fish that inhabit the shallows including mullet and garfish. The fish can be very hard to spot but they can't camouflage their shadows.

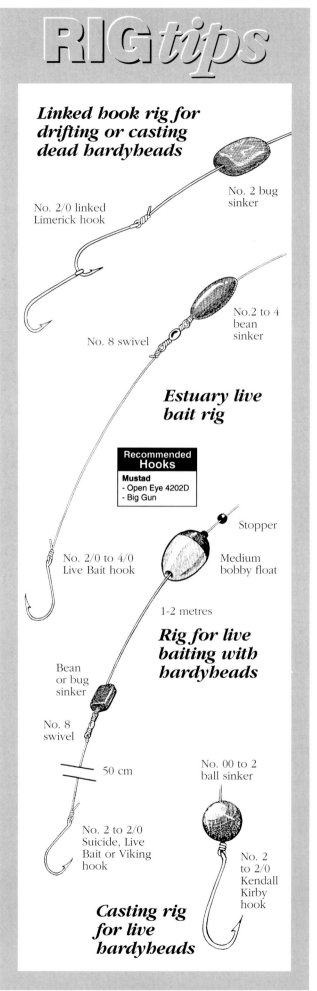

Linked hook rig for drifting or casting dead hardyheads

No. 2/0 linked Limerick hook

No. 2 bug sinker

No.2 to 4 bean sinker

No. 8 swivel

Estuary live bait rig

Recommended Hooks
Mustad
- Open Eye 4202D
- Big Gun

No. 2/0 to 4/0 Live Bait hook

Stopper

Medium bobby float

1-2 metres

Rig for live baiting with hardyheads

Bean or bug sinker

No. 8 swivel

50 cm

No. 2 to 2/0 Suicide, Live Bait or Viking hook

No. 00 to 2 ball sinker

No. 2 to 2/0 Kendall Kirby hook

Casting rig for live hardyheads

Herrings

Live herring in a bait tank.

Herring are a common estuary and near shore bait fish with a number of species found around Australia. They are found from Sydney north with big populations in many coastal rivers. In the tropics they are an important bait fish with anglers using them to catch a wide variety of fish.

Sometimes called sardines, shad or cat tails the herring are often found in large schools.

Once located, big numbers of these baits can be captured quickly and either kept alive in a bait tank or dropped onto ice for use as fresh or cut bait.

Herring are different to most other bait fish as they don't take baited hooks yet are very aggressive little hunters themselves.

They feed on small planktonic shrimp and can often be seen flicking on the surface as they attack their prey.

Where to Find Them

Herring gather in tidal eddies, along current lines, in deep holes and around jetties. Anywhere with plenty of current is likely to set up a feeding area for the herring.

The low current eddies where two creeks or where rivers meet is always likely. The same applies to shallow banks that fall away into coastal lakes and lagoons. These spots, often known as 'steps', hold big schools of herring, particularly on the run-in tide.

Herring are attracted by lights and often gather in very big numbers around bridge pylons and jetties at night.

Herring are located in several ways. Knowing where to find them helps establish the most likely spots but keen eyes and an echo sounder can be an important part of the search.

Using a sounder is the easy way of finding the fish when working from a boat. Gathering in dense schools, the herring will show up clearly on the screen. They

can also be seen flicking on the surface. Underneath the few fish flicking there will often be quite large numbers of herring. The other characteristic of the fish is to flick over on their sides as they swim along within a school. The fish flicking over sends out a very distinct silver flash which can be easily seen by an observant angler.

How to Catch Them

As earlier stated, herring do not usually take a baited hook, but their aggressive nature can be exploited by using small bait jigs which they attack with great gusto.

Bait jigs with size No.8, 10 or 12 hooks are ideal and it is common for the bait jigs to catch a herring on every hook if they are feeding readily. The very tiny, No.12 size hook bait jigs can be used to catch quite small herring which can be important for some types of estuary angling.

In Queensland and the Northern Territory, cast nets are used on herring with great success. The herring

How to Use Them

Live herring are a deadly bait on predatory fish. The important part about using them is to position the hook in the bait so that it does not hurt the bait yet is well positioned to hook whatever takes the bait.

Herring can be injured easily by careless hook placement and they also do not carry large or heavy gauge hooks very well. The answer is to use smaller sized hooks and those of lighter gauge for best results.

Two of the best hooks are the Mustad 4174 KEBR and the Daiichi 3000 series. Hook size depends on the size of the bait fish and the size of the fish expected to be caught.

Hooks from 2/0 to 6/0 are appropriate with 4/0 being standard for most situations.

The best way to present a herring is to push the hook in through the underside of the lower jaw and bring it out through the top of the nose just a little in front of the eyes. Do not push the hook through the area between the herring's eyes, this will kill it instantly.

Hooked in this manner the bait can be worked in any current and still stay alive. It can also be drifted and will remain virtually snag free as the fish swims along keeping the hook point away from any snags.

When fishing with bobby floats or similar rigs or if fishing in areas of low current flow, the bait can be

hooked through the shoulder area. When doing this, ensure the hook stays away from the lateral line, puncturing this will kill the fish.

Herring take a little extra care but they are an excellent bait and being a natural target they will catch just about every predatory estuary fish.

Herring rigged with hook placements for live bait.

Profile of herring.

Estuary live bait rig

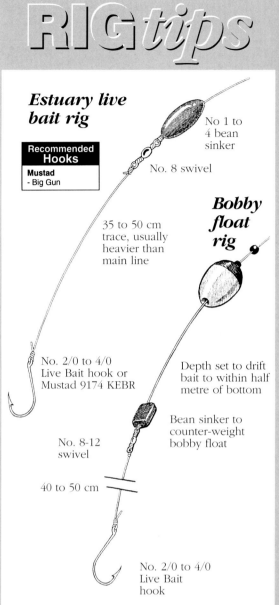

Recommended Hooks

Mustad
- Big Gun

No 1 to 4 bean sinker

No. 8 swivel

35 to 50 cm trace, usually heavier than main line

No. 2/0 to 4/0 Live Bait hook or Mustad 9174 KEBR

No. 8-12 swivel

40 to 50 cm

Bobby float rig

Depth set to drift bait to within half metre of bottom

Bean sinker to counter-weight bobby float

No. 2/0 to 4/0 Live Bait hook

are netted along the edges of banks and drop-offs and from holes and tidal corners in mangrove creeks. Being a school fish, enough herring can sometimes be caught for a days fishing with one or two well placed throws of the cast net.

Handling

Herring can be kept alive in a bait tank although they are not particularly hardy and can be easily damaged by rough handling. They do not stay alive for long periods in captivity either, losing their scales and often dying after six to eight hours.

This is more than long enough for a fishing session but it makes keeping the bait alive overnight more difficult. From experience not all the baits die if kept overnight in some form of keeper but mortality can be high.

Herring are extremely important in tropical creek fishing.

Mackerel *slimy*

Game fish find slimy mackerel irresistible as bait.

Slimy mackerel *(Scomber australasicus)* also known as common or blue mackerel are an important bait fish around much of the temperate Australian coast. Growing to over a kilogram and being common at around 400 grams the fish are both fun to catch and make great bait used live, fresh or preserved.

Slimy mackerel are bright, shiny, oily and seductively attractive to other fish. The fish also turn up in all sorts of sizes from about the size of a pilchard upwards. No matter what size they are, slimy mackerel are a magic bait for big fish.

The size variation of the mackerel often dictates their use as bait. The larger sizes are first rate game fish bait for marlin and tuna while the smaller sizes are productive on almost any predatory fish.

Where to Find Them

Slimy mackerel are common offshore particularly around shallow ocean reefs and kelp areas. They regularly enter large bays and harbours where they provide great sport around piers and jetties. In many estuaries they feed over areas of ribbon weed or in tidal eddies near the entrance to the system.

Slimy mackerel schools tend to congregate in the same spots and regular anglers can learn their haunts fairly quickly.

Offshore, recognised bait grounds are the most common place to find slimy mackerel but they are often encountered by sounding around offshore reefs out to 50 metres.

How to Catch Them

Once located, slimy mackerel are fairly easy to catch. Two methods work best.

A light line rigged with a small split shot set about 20 cm from a No.8 to No.4 size Long Shank hook and baited with a small fish strip, works extremely well. The line is usually a 3 to 4 kg handline if fished from a boat or a 2 to 3 kg line if fishing with a rod.

How to Use Them

Slimy mackerel are a definitive live bait, almost everything likes to eat them. It is mostly a matter of matching the bait size to the target fish.

The medium to large size mackerel are brilliant game fish baits, as well as being prized baits for Spanish mackerel (no relation), yellowtail kingfish, mulloway and other predators.

Slimy mackerel also make first class cut and strip baits for bream, flathead, mulloway, snapper and reef fish. The only problem is the fish do not freeze well and need to be used fresh. Slimy mackerel soften markedly once frozen and don't make very good bait once thawed.

The best way to handle mackerel to be used as strip baits is to drop them straight onto ice and then use them as needed during the fishing session.

When using slimy mackerel alive the best way to hook them is through the bony part of the snout in the clear area just in front of the eyes. This enables the bait to swim freely while presenting the hook in the best spot to snare an attacking fish.

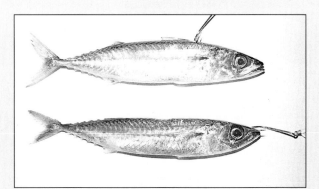
Hooking arrangements for live slimy mackerel.

Slimy mackerel in bait tank.

Slimy mackerel should be kept on ice to maintain freshness and firmness as bait.

In estuaries and on shallow offshore bait grounds, berley helps markedly in attracting the mackerel and keeping them feeding in the angling area. The best berley is wet bread with a few pulped pilchards mixed in or just pulped fish mash from a berley bucket.

The second method of capture is with a bait jig. The slimy mackerel is itself an aggressive feeder on small fish and shrimps and will readily attack most small bait jigs. The bait jigs are used to catch the fish on the deeper ocean reefs where the schools are located with the depth sounder and the bait jigs are dropped into the 'show'. The bait jigs also work well in shallow areas when the fish are feeding actively.

Handling

Slimy mackerel are highly sensitive to rough handling and if wanted for live bait should simply be shaken off the hook without actually touching the fish. If this is not possible handle them gently and then drop them into the tank.

Slimy mackerel use lots of oxygen and the bait tank needs to have water pumping through it to sustain these bait fish.

Points of Note

Apart from being a top bait fish, slimy mackerel are great fun to catch and are quite good eating. They can also be smoked to produce a quality product which is as good as any smoked fish.

As a bait fish though, slimy mackerel are about the best thing that swims. They are also able to be kept and transported in live bait tanks which makes them very versatile.

Slimy mackerel caught using a bait jig.

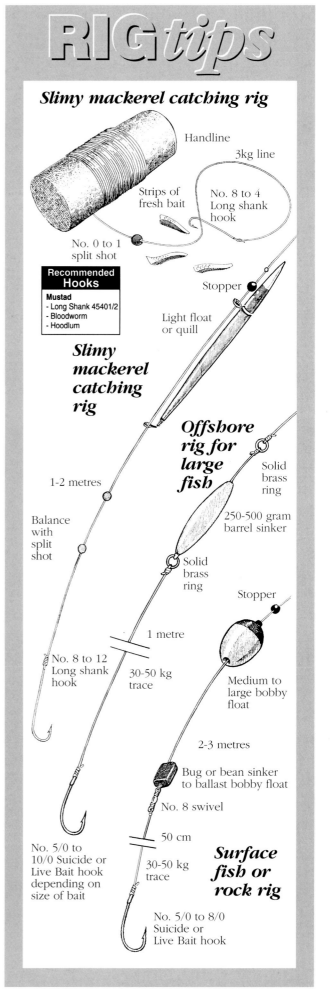

Slimy mackerel catching rig

Handline

3kg line

Strips of fresh bait

No. 8 to 4 Long shank hook

No. 0 to 1 split shot

Recommended Hooks
Mustad
- Long Shank 45401/2
- Bloodworm
- Hoodlum

Stopper

Light float or quill

Slimy mackerel catching rig

1-2 metres

Balance with split shot

Offshore rig for large fish

Solid brass ring

250-500 gram barrel sinker

Solid brass ring

Stopper

Medium to large bobby float

1 metre

30-50 kg trace

No. 8 to 12 Long shank hook

2-3 metres

Bug or bean sinker to ballast bobby float

No. 8 swivel

50 cm

30-50 kg trace

No. 5/0 to 10/0 Suicide or Live Bait hook depending on size of bait

Surface fish or rock rig

No. 5/0 to 8/0 Suicide or Live Bait hook

Selection of typical minnows and gudgeons.

In Australian freshwater fishing, minnows are usually any fish used for bait. The title 'minnow' is a bit of a misnomer. These small, native fish are from several families mostly galaxids, jollytails, smelt, hardyheads and gudgeons.

All make good bait and are attractive to almost all the freshwater sportfish.

In some Victorian and Tasmanian lakes these fish are the primary food in the lakes, making them the bait of choice for most anglers.

Galaxids grow to 100 mm and form the largest family of fish in temperate and cool southern waters. These are the main baits available in Victoria and Tasmania. Jollytails, a larger galaxid which grows to 160 mm overlaps into the warm Murray/Darling River system and form part of the diet of Murray cod and other larger species.

Gudgeons form the main block of species in New South Wales and southern Victoria. Gudgeons are also important bait items for bass in east coast streams.

Other small fish like smelt, small tench, roach and redfin can be added to make quite a long list of available small bait fish.

Where to Find Them

The general rule is to only catch and use bait fish in the same waterway, don't trans-locate them. (See Points of Note). The best place to find small bait fish is around weed beds and around over-hanging bankside cover. Often the small fish can be observed darting about or moving around an area in small schools.

They are fairly easy to find at night. Walking around the waterway with a bright light will often reveal schools of bait fish. They also hang about popular fishing areas where bait and more usually berley provides plenty of food for the smaller fish.

How to Catch Them

By far the easiest way to catch live minnows is to trap them. There are many live bait traps available in tackle shops using either the wire drum or one way funnel system. The collapsible shrimp box type traps are also good for this.

The traps rely on some form of bait to attract the minnows, usually bread, corn or chopped worms and the small fish find their way into the trap and are unable to find their way out.

In flowing streams, always ensure the entrance funnel faces down current and is directly in line with the flow of the water. Feeding fish always face into the current no matter how big or small they happen to be.

Other methods of catch-

How to Use Them

When using live fish for bait, keep in mind the size of fish being sought. If small fish are expected, use small bait fish. It doesn't matter so much with cod but it does on stream trout and in many lakes.

The longer, thin bodied type baits seem to be more attractive to the fish than the more thick bodied types. With thick bodied baits like tench, roach and redfin, the key is to use very small baits.

When hooking live baits, the best method is usually through the upper jaw. This is particularly so in running water as any other hook placement will kill or spin the bait.

Anglers drifting baits under a float often hook the fish above the lateral line just behind the shoulder, about the start of the dorsal fin. This presents the bait in an attractive manner to any interested fish.

Some trout anglers hook two galaxids together through the base of the tail. The two fish struggling together seems to really excite the trout into attacking the bait.

The only problem with this double fish system is that the bait tire and lose their attractiveness quickly and it takes twice as many bait fish to work the system.

Most freshwater live baits are fished below a bubble float or something similar. Some trout anglers fish their baits in free swimming mode when boat fishing in open water.

Anglers looking for cod and yellowbelly use a short trace of 30 cm to a swivel and then a heavy sinker to secure the live bait in a selected location.

Twin galaxids on a hook make a great bait that has plenty of action and attraction.

eons & smelt

ing bait include using a dip net around weed beds and other cover. This is particularly effective at night when the schools of bait fish are not as skittish as during the day.

Points of Note
It should also be noted that it is illegal to use ANY live freshwater fish as bait in New South Wales.

One of the great problems in Australian freshwater fishing has been the introduction of unwanted pest fish into waterways and impoundments. Many of these introductions are thought to have occurred through anglers using small, live fish for bait and then releasing whatever fish were left, into the waterway.

It is also illegal to use carp in almost all waterways of Australia, although nearly all waters now contain them anyway.

All small fish make good bait and are attractive to most freshwater sportfish.

Above: Trout and salmon both feed heavily on minnows in most lakes and rivers.
Below: The Bull head minnow is a popular live bait in Victoria that accounts for many large trout.

RIGtips

Unweighted drift rig for trout

No. 6 to 4 Baitholder hook

Recommended Hooks
Mustad
- Big Red

Minnow rig

An ideal rig for all freshwater fish which is designed for use in deep water, mainly lakes.

Use a bubble float with a valve rubber stopper and hook two live minnows or galaxids through the tail.

To make a valve rubber stopper thread the line through a short piece of bicycle valve rubber and back through once more. Pull on the line both sides of the stopper. When the line straightens the rubber wraps tightly around the line forming a stopper.

Lumo and light plastic tube can be used in light lines but need to be placed in hot water, coffee, tea etc before pulling the line tight.

Mudeyes

The mudeye is the larval stage of the dragonfly. It spends this part of its life cycle as an aquatic predator, and it hunts other aquatic insects, tadpoles and worms. The mudeye is usually 1 to 3 cm in length and dark brown to pale green in colour.

Just as there are many species of dragonflies, there are likewise a similar number of different types of mudeyes. The two most common being the large 'couta' mudeye and the 'spider' or 'bug' mudeye.

Mudeyes are probably the best bait available for trout fishing, and when fished correctly will yield good catches both in rivers and lakes. They can also be trolled behind Ford Fender or Cowbell type attractors with devastating effect.

Where to Find Them

Mudeyes inhabit the still water of ponds, dams and lakes. They live in the weeds, under rocks, submerged trees and other cover and hunt other aquatic animals.

The waters inhabited by mudeyes must be free of agricultural chemicals as they are highly sensitive to even tiny amounts of pesticides. When searching for mudeyes it will become readily apparent that some dams have absolutely no mudeyes while others have plenty. This is usually a result of chemicals in the water or lack of suitable cover.

The time to collect mudeyes is late winter, spring and early summer. Once the warmer weather arrives the mudeyes emerge as dragonflies, and the bait will no longer be available.

Small ponds and dams are the ideal place to look for mudeyes but they can also be found in most of the major impoundments and can be caught in several ways to add to the bait supply.

Fishing live mudeyes under bubble floats around flooded trees is a prime place to pursue trout.

How to Catch Them

The best method of extracting mudeyes from a pond or farm dam is to push a 'mudeye net' through the weeds, scooping or dragging it near the bottom to collect plenty of weed and debris with each scoop.

How To Use Them

The secret to using mudeyes is to ensure that the mudeye is as lively and as natural as possible in the water.

This is achieved by using a very small hook, size No.10 to No.14 and hooking the mudeye through the base of the wings. Some anglers attach the mudeye by placing the hook into the bait through the anal vent and then bending the bait around the bend of the hook with the point of the hook emerging from the underbelly area. The rest of the hook is eased inside the mudeye and only the point is exposed.

Mudeyes are most effectively used under a float of some sort, usually a bubble type. A stopper is used to set the depth the mudeye can drift down. A tiny No.14 black swivel is placed about half a metre from the bait and this is the only weight used in the rig.

The line above the float should be greased so it will float on the surface and not sink and snag on the bottom while waiting for a take.

Trout tend to take a mudeye gently, so set the rig with some slack line or an open bail arm to allow the fish an unhindered run when it takes the bait.

Mudeyes can also be trolled very successfully about half a metre behind Ford Fender or Cowbell type attractors.

There are two methods of rigging the bait for trolling. The technique uses a long shank, round bend, fine gauge, wide gape fly hook of a size to suit the mudeyes available.

The first method is to pre-rig half a dozen traces with a hook. A stainless steel sewing needle then has the trace threaded through the eye and the needle is passed straight through the bait from the anal vent out through the middle of the head.

The mudeye is then eased down onto the hook and the bend of the hook and the hook point remain outside the bait. The trace is then tied to the attractor at the desired length.

In the second method, the point of the hook is inserted right into the mouth and then pushed down the centre of the bait, carefully threading the mudeye around the shank of the hook. The point of the hook comes out exactly dead centre in the lower abdomen. The hook is then pulled very gently so that the hook eye and knot are pulled into the mudeyes head.

This rig is then trolled very slowly in likely areas.

Above: The best way to hook a live mudeye is through the wings with a small fly hook.
Below: Rigged mudeye.

The mudeye net is then up-ended on the bank close to the edge and the mudeyes extracted from the catch.

The mudeye net can be made or purchased from tackle shops in southern areas. The nets are made with a solid handle and frame with a fine but strong mesh. It features a flat bottom on the jaws of the net to allow it to be swept along the bottom of the ponds.

A good dam can produce 10 or 12 mudeyes per sweep of the net and a lot of bait can be harvested in a mornings work.

On big dams, mudeyes can be located by netting in weed areas just as on ponds. The mudeyes can also be found by lifting sunken timber and examining it. The mudeyes will be found clinging to the underside of the timber and in any cracks or fissures in the timber.

Alternatively, a hessian bag can be rolled and tied into a bundle around a stone and set amongst heavy sunken timber. The bag can be recovered every couple of days and unwrapped. The mudeyes will be found seeking cover in the spaces between the wraps of the bag.

Handling

If mudeyes are being caught and used over a couple of days then they only need to be stored in a small six pack type polystyrene esky. This type of container will hold up to 100 baits.

For long term storage the mudeyes must be kept cool and in total darkness. Once the temperature rises they rapidly develop into dragonflies and hatch ending their usefulness as bait.

The key is to handle them very carefully for future use. Use a polystyrene six pack esky and place a layer of damp foam rubber on the bottom and put a layer of mudeyes on top. Another piece of damp foam is then softly placed on top followed by another layer of mudeyes.

This process is continued

Trout are the prime candidate when fishing with mudeyes.

until the esky is full. The baits are then stored in a fridge set at its lowest level, just cool, not ice cold. This will send the mudeyes into hibernation and they can be used as needed for the next four months or so.

Some mortality will occur using this method, but about 70 per cent will survive.

For shorter storage periods the mudeyes can be placed in a large esky, allowing about eight litres of water per dozen mudeyes. The water needs to be changed every 10 days or so. The esky is stored somewhere dark and cool, such as under the house. Stored this way, the mudeyes will last about two months.

Points of Note

Mudeyes are hypersensitive to any forms of insecticide including personal repellent that may be on the anglers hands.

Always ensure that no suncream, insect spray or repellent is used when catching and sorting the mudeyes.

The same thing applies at home when sorting and preparing the mudeyes for storage. Any exposure to any level of pesticide will kill all the hard won mudeyes. The same care is needed while using them on a fishing trip.

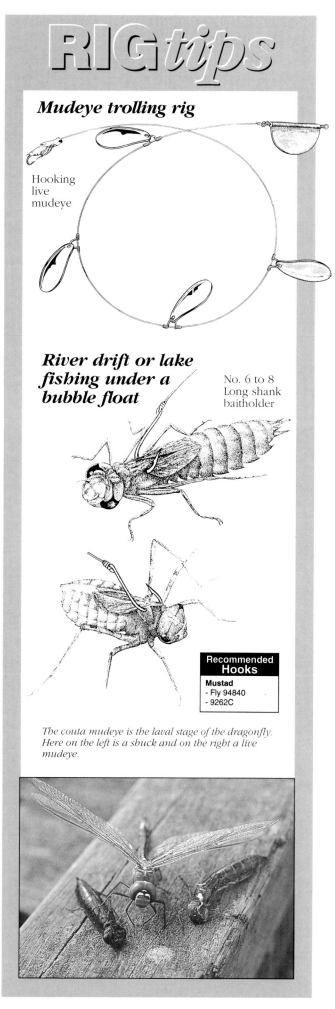

RIGtips

Mudeye trolling rig

Hooking live mudeye

River drift or lake fishing under a bubble float

No. 6 to 8 Long shank baitholder

Recommended Hooks

Mustad
- Fly 94840
- 9262C

The couta mudeye is the laval stage of the dragonfly. Here on the left is a shuck and on the right a live mudeye.

Mullet

Mullet are a very common and popular bait fish found right around the country. From little poddies through to the biggest sizes, mullet make great bait. The only trick is to match the size of the mullet with the size of the fish you want to catch. Mullet are distributed worldwide as a specie and they are common on almost every continent.

They are a hardy fish and provide great fishing as well as good bait. Being easy to catch, keen to feed and common around piers and jetties makes them a popular fish with many anglers.

For young anglers, mullet are usually one of the first fish they are likely to catch from a pier or jetty.

Apart from bait, the larger mullet are of variable eating quality with sand mullet being very tasty but some species having a distinctive weedy flavour. All the larger mullet are good fighters and excellent sport on light tackle.

Where to Find Them

Anglers catching mullet for bait are usually seeking the smaller size versions for most situations, with a few mulloway and barra anglers keen to use fish up to 500 grams for bait on big fish.

Mullet are usually found over sandflats, near weed beds, along sandy banks particularly near picnic grounds, in shallow coastal lagoons, around wharves and jetties and near outlet pipes for fish co-operatives, cane mills and similar areas.

Mullet are surface feeders

Kids really enjoy catching mullet.

in many areas and they are often easy to spot using sunglasses with polarised lenses.

Mullet use the same feeding locations over very long periods of time and once these places are learned it is fairly easy to catch enough for bait.

How to Catch Them

There are a number of methods for catching mullet, bait traps, cast and drag nets or by using small hooks and bait.

Most of the mullet caught in traps are small, from 5 to 15 cm, and they are ideal for most estuary live bait work.

Trapping involves using either a perspex tube type bait trap, one of the fine mesh box types or an improvised version of the same thing. Traps are baited with bread and left in the shallows.

The area is usually 'seeded' with a little mulched bread to attract and hold the mullet while they find their way into the trap.

The basic rule is, if the

Large dusky flathead are highly attracted to well presented live mullet.

mullet won't come to the berley, they won't enter the trap either.

The best place to lay the trap is in the quite end of a bay or in areas where there are already plenty of small mullet feeding. When learning, watch where others successfully catch the mullet, it can take out a lot of the guesswork.

Mullet of all sizes from very small to over a kilogram can be caught using standard fishing tackle.

The rig is usually a small

How to Use Them

Live mullet are top bait for all manner of predatory fish. In the tropics barramundi, fingermark bream, mangrove jack, cod, trevally, queenfish and a host of others will all take them. In temperate waters mulloway, flathead, tailor, salmon, bream and other surface fish are the main takers.

In the tropics, fishing a live mullet by suspending it under a float and drifting it by a likely snag or rock bar is always likely to yield big fish. The same method with the bait suspended near the bottom, is used to fish live mullet from breakwalls for big mulloway and flathead.

Anglers who use live mullet while drifting from a boat usually hook them through the top and bottom jaw to facilitate a good presentation. The same method should also be used when fishing in a strong current.

In low current or slow drift situations, hooking the bait through the area of the first dorsal fin is a good way to present the bait. Just remember not to put the hook anywhere near the fish's lateral line. Drifting or fishing with dead, small mullet can also be highly productive. Using double linked hooks is about the best method of presentation. Larger mullet can be used for strip baits and it is best to scale the fish before filleting and cutting the fillet into the appropriate strips.

Hook sizes for estuary live baiting are 3/0 to 5/0 and when working big baits for mulloway hooks from 6/0 to 10/0 are used depending on the size of the bait.

Above: Two hook rig for mullet is excellent when targeting large fish like flathead and mulloway.
Below: Small mullet rigged for trolling.

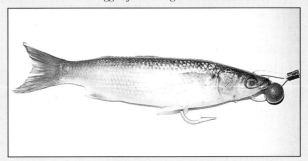

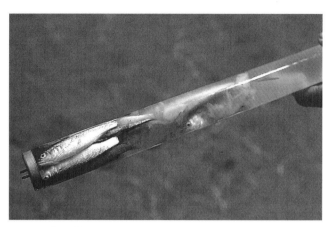

Very small mullet, only between 50-90 mm in length, as caught here in a fluoro tube, are ideal to be used live for flathead.

float of some kind fitted with lead if necessary and a No.12 to No.8 Long Shank, Eastern Estuary or Suicide hook. Lead is only used if the fish are feeding at depth. If the fish are in the shallows, use no lead at all.

The best baits are bread, dough, worm pieces, prawn pieces and maggots.

The area is berleyed with bread and the mullet are caught using the baited hook and float. Long lightweight rods like those used for estuary luderick are ideal for this type of fishing.

Watching the float intently and knowing when to strike is part of the fun of catching mullet. The fish bite readily and are struck as the float is pulled under.

In northern states where cast nets and bait nets are legal, catching mullet is often fast and easier than for southerners working with baited hooks. The mullet schools once found can be caught with a cast net, particularly in shallow water less than 30 cm deep.

Bait nets can also be hauled through the shallows in areas where the mullet are likely to be or can be seen. When using nets, only take the bait needed, there is no point putting too many baits in one tank.

Handling

Mullet make great live bait, and most anglers keep them alive in a bait tank, cooler or

bucket until they are ready to fish with them. The only essential is to keep up the oxygen supply in the container with either regular changes of water, an aerator or the use of a bait tank if on a vessel.

Mullet are robust and handle easily and without damage if reasonable care is taken. Like all live baits though, the more care you take with the bait the better they present to the fish.

Points of Note

Mullet are used extensively as trolling baits for marlin, sailfish and Spanish mackerel. Mostly medium sized fish around half a kilo are preferred and a range of rigs and tricks are used to make the bait swim straight through the water.

The key is the removal of the fish's spine using a sharpened piece of stainless steel tubing. With the spine removed and a 30 gram ball sinker secured under the bait's chin, the mullet will swim along at about 4 knots in a very seductive manner.

Learning how to rig them takes a little bit of time but with modern monofilament trace and crimping pliers, the baits can be rigged quickly and without fuss in a few minutes.

Trolled rigged mullet work best with really fresh bait and the only way to get them peerlessly fresh is to catch them yourself.

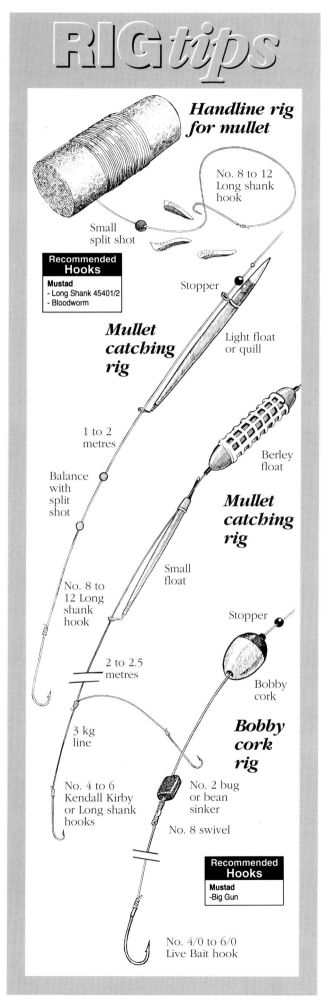

RIG *tips*

Handline rig for mullet

No. 8 to 12 Long shank hook

Small split shot

Recommended Hooks
Mustad
- Long Shank 45401/2
- Bloodworm

Stopper

Mullet catching rig

Light float or quill

1 to 2 metres

Balance with split shot

Berley float

Mullet catching rig

Small float

No. 8 to 12 Long shank hook

Stopper

2 to 2.5 metres

Bobby cork

3 kg line

Bobby cork rig

No. 4 to 6 Kendall Kirby or Long shank hooks

No. 2 bug or bean sinker

No. 8 swivel

Recommended Hooks
Mustad
-Big Gun

No. 4/0 to 6/0 Live Bait hook

Mussels

Noted whiting fisherman Bernie Bliss gathers mussels from a channel marker in Corio Bay with a gardening implement.

M ussels *(Mytilus planulatus)* are a very common and easily harvested bait particularly in the southern parts of the continent.

Like most shellfish they are eaten by a wide variety of fish. They are also grown commercially for human consumption. Mussels collected for bait can also be eaten but make sure they come from unpolluted waters or a stomach upset can result.

Being a natural bait and part of the diet of many grazing feeders the mussel is always a fairly popular bait. Fish like bream, King George whiting, leatherjackets, drummer, dart, morwong, tarwhine, snapper and parrotfish will all eat mussels.

At times mussels are the number one bait for King George whiting in Victoria and are harvested vigorously by keen whiting anglers.

Where to Find Them

The distinctive black and purple shell of the mussel makes them unmistakable from other shellfish. They also gather in big clusters in their preferred area. Places like the pylons of wharves, jetties and bridges, over shallow rocks, along foreshore areas and rock walls. They also gather on mooring lines and floating navigational structures.

Mussels are common in the southern half of the continent from about Sydney south with large populations in southern New South Wales and Victoria.

In most areas they are easily located around wharves and rocky foreshores with the only problem being how to retrieve them from some spots.

How to Collect Them

Mussels can be torn away from their clusters with a gloved hand if access is available to them by boat or land. They come away fairly easily but protection for the hands is essential.

Jetty based anglers often use a stout rake to lift them off their feeding station on the pylons. These mussel rakes have a semicircle of chicken wire fitted around the rake to collect any mus-

How to Use Them

Mussels are not a particularly tough bait and care needs to be taken putting them on the hook, so they remain in place during both casting and fishing.

The way to put the mussel on the hook is to pass the point of the hook through the tough feeding syphon which looks black and is in the centre of the bait. The rest of the mussel tissue is then threaded several times onto the hook. Many anglers place a half hitch onto the top part of the bait and around the hook to help secure the bait.

Hook sizes used are generally No.6 to 1/0 depending on the species of fish being sought.

Open mussel and rigged bait.

Above: Leatherjackets feed keenly on mussels.
Right: Mussels are usually found in large numbers.

sels that fall away loosely as the rake tears them off the pylons.

Where close access is available they can also be cut away easily with a stout knife. Just be careful to cut under the clumps to free them rather than forcing the blade against the shells which can cause cuts to the angler if the knife suddenly slips. The trick is to lift them off in clumps once a few mussels have been removed.

Mussels are always easiest to locate and harvest at low tide.

Handling

Mussels are mostly used fresh but they do freeze and salt very well.

Mussels will stay alive for three or four days in the shell once harvested. Provided they are kept in a cool spot.

Anglers who want to harvest a bait supply and use it later can open the shells by cutting them at the back hinge with a stout knife. The meaty shellfish within is removed in one piece and placed in a take-away food container partly filled with seawater. When sufficient bait has been extracted for a days fishing the water level is topped up to cover the mussels and it is then placed in the freezer.

Mussels stored in this manner will thaw out in good condition.

The mussels can also be dropped into a jar after shelling and covered liberally with coarse salt. This preserves and toughens the flesh but it remains highly acceptable to the fish.

The jar of salted mussels is kept in the refrigerator until needed for bait.

Points of Note

When using mussels and similar soft baits anglers who use long soft actioned rods can often cast the bait better and catch more fish than anglers using more conventional fast tapered rods.

The soft, slow actioned rods tend not to stress or throw the bait off the hook while the same rods also tend to let the fish eat the bait more readily than faster, stiffer rods.

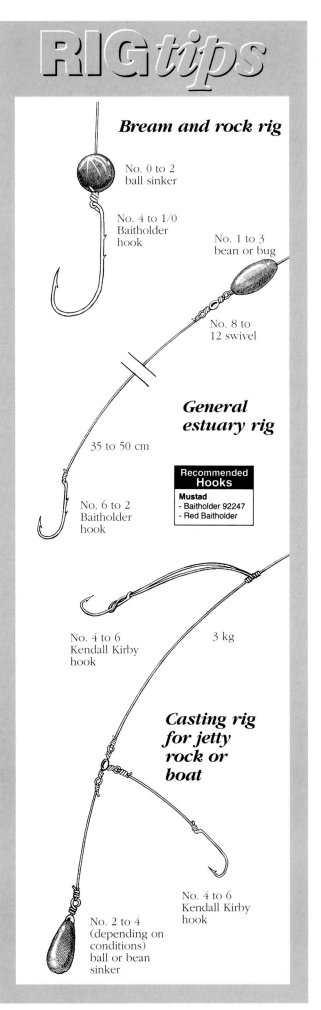

RIGtips

Bream and rock rig

No. 0 to 2 ball sinker

No. 4 to 1/0 Baitholder hook

No. 1 to 3 bean or bug

No. 8 to 12 swivel

General estuary rig

35 to 50 cm

No. 6 to 2 Baitholder hook

Recommended Hooks
Mustad
- Baitholder 92247
- Red Baitholder

No. 4 to 6 Kendall Kirby hook

3 kg

Casting rig for jetty rock or boat

No. 4 to 6 Kendall Kirby hook

No. 2 to 4 (depending on conditions) ball or bean sinker

Octopus

Octopus is a popular bait with many off-shore anglers although they are also very good bait for estuary mulloway.

Their size varies enormously from tiny to very large animals of 5 or 6 kg.

They are a tough bait, resistant to pickers but they can also be a difficult bait to rig and work in some circumstances.

As with many fish and crustaceans once regarded only as bait the octopus is now considered as something of a gourmet dish and is found on a wide variety of restaurant menus. This means that a once cheap bait is now expensive or comparatively so.

Where to Find Them

Small octopus are the most popular for bait. This size occi is mostly caught by prawn trawlers operating in ocean waters and is purchased from bait shops or fish mongers. Larger size octopus turn up in estuaries and around the ocean rocks.

Estuary octopus live in weed beds usually in burrows surrounded by a collection of opened oyster shells. They commonly inhabit kelp beds and the cavities of rocky shelves and crevices. In some areas they are often found under large rocks in the intertidal zone.

Ocean species inhabit breakwaters, rocky foreshores, rock pools and almost any rocky or weedy areas in the intertidal zones. Again kelp beds tend to be very popular.

How to Catch Them

Octopuses are an active and very successful hunter, preying on crabs, shrimp, shellfish, crayfish and other crustaceans. They also seek shelter of almost any kind so long as it offers them somewhere to hide.

Octopus can be caught by using multi-prong jags baited with a crab lowered into a hole or crevice where they are likely to live.

Some very ingenious baited octopus rigs are available and these incorporate the use of a crab to make them work. The rig is baited with a crab and fished in areas likely to yield an octopus. When the octopus attacks the crab it is impaled on the sharp hooks on the end of the jig. Octopus can also be trapped in small traps baited with crabs or fish heads.

At night, they can be found prowling around the weed beds, rock pools or along rocky shorelines. A powerful light or torch is used and the occi is caught with a prawn scoop net or spear.

The octopus' demand for shelter can also be used to trap them. Pieces of PVC tube with an end cap attached can be placed discretely in areas like weed beds or along rocky shorelines and recovered early the next morning. Often an octopus will move in overnight.

These PVC tubes can also be weighted and marked with small floats if required.

Handling

Most octopus are used as dead bait and live ones are almost impossible to keep in any container.

The easiest way to handle them is to drop them straight onto an ice slurry which kills them very quickly and humanely.

If keeping them alive for mulloway or kingfish bait, use a container with a very tight fitting lid.

Octopus and occi leg rigged for bait.

Octopus is very tough bait and will stay firmly on the hook no matter how it is rigged.

How to Use Them

Small octopus are used either whole or in strips and are excellent bait for offshore bottom fish.

The larger octopus are either used whole for large mulloway and similar reef feeders or the tentacles are used one by one to make very attractive strip baits for snapper, mulloway, kingfish and other reef dwelling species. The head section of the occi is usually discarded and not used as bait.

On large octopus the inner tendon part of the tentacle is often used as bait. This is removed from the suckers and skin tissue by first removing the tentacles and then dropping each tentacle into boiling water, leaving it in the water for about 10 seconds. The tendon is then removed from the suckers and tissue by pulling the tendon with one hand while holding the outer layer with some towelling or a sugar bag.

The end result is a snow white strip of bait which is excellent on kingfish and can also be trolled if necessary.

Two hook gangs are often used on both whole small occi and occi legs to get the best bait presentation.

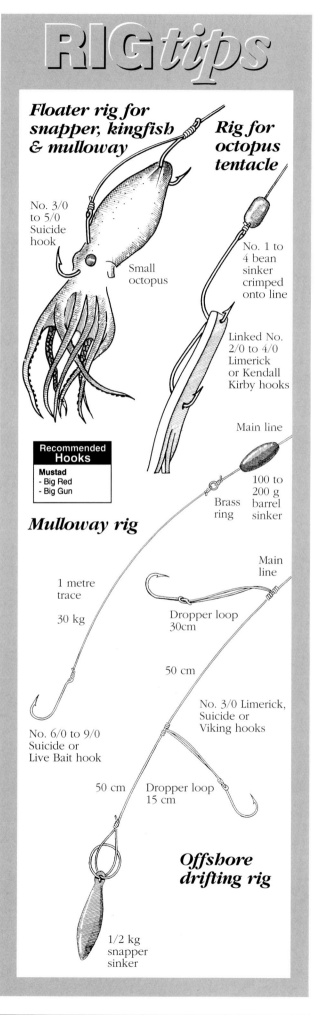

Floater rig for snapper, kingfish & mulloway

Rig for octopus tentacle

No. 3/0 to 5/0 Suicide hook

Small octopus

No. 1 to 4 bean sinker crimped onto line

Linked No. 2/0 to 4/0 Limerick or Kendall Kirby hooks

Main line

Recommended Hooks

Mustad
- Big Red
- Big Gun

Mulloway rig

100 to 200 g barrel sinker

Brass ring

Main line

1 metre trace

30 kg

Dropper loop 30cm

50 cm

No. 3/0 Limerick, Suicide or Viking hooks

No. 6/0 to 9/0 Suicide or Live Bait hook

50 cm

Dropper loop 15 cm

Offshore drifting rig

1/2 kg snapper sinker

Yellowtail kingfish feed keenly on octopus.

Points of Note

When gathering octopus for bait some of the very small octopus are often the deadly blue ringed variety which are highly toxic and should not be handled under any circumstances.

Octopus have a parrot-like beak at the point on their underside where all eight arms meet. Do not allow any octopus the chance to bite the angler with this beak.

Handle all octopus with care and leave the tiny ones alone. Any octopus that shows electric blue colours when handled should be dropped immediately.

Profile of octopus.

Pilchards

Of all the bait fish that anglers rely on, nothing is as important as pilchards. Pilchards are used for just about everything but have particular importance for anglers seeking tailor, flathead, salmon, snapper, mackerel, yellowfin and coral dwellers.

Pilchards *(Sardinops neopilchardus)* grow to about 29 cm but are more commonly caught at 15 cm. They are best recognised by the line of dark spots along the body. Their body is soft and oily making them very attractive to fish.

The pilchard is a vital link in the recreational fishing process.

Where To Find Them

Pilchards are commonly found in coastal waters of

Berleying or cubing with pilchards is a very successful way to fish for yellowfin tuna.

Australia's southern half, where they form large schools. Commercially packaged pilchards sold in bait shops have quite a story to tell. The humble pilchard actually constitutes a huge industry for commercial fishermen around Albany and Fremantle in the southern corner of Western Australia.

Here the pilchards are caught in small purse seine nets and processed on the spot. The fish are frozen within minutes of leaving the water. Some of these boats are equipped to keep the pilchards alive in pens until they are ready to process them.

How to Catch Them

While most anglers use the commercial product, pilchards are often caught on bait jigs at sea. The pilchards are a different specie to the WA model but they are still great bait. They don't stay alive very long in the bait tank but fished fresh they are deadly on mackerel, snapper and tuna.

Pilchards will also gather in the lights of vessels moored or drifting at night and again can be caught on bait jigs.

Catching pilchards is

How to Use Them

The classic method of fishing with pilchards is on a three or four hook gang. This rig is deadly on aggressive feeders like tailor, salmon, mackerel and coral trout.

The rig is made up of 3/0, 4/0 or 5/0 hooks, usually tinned Limericks or Kendall Kirby patterns. The hook sizes chosen are usually to suite the size of the bait rather than to suit the size of the fish being caught.

As a rule three 4/0 hooks ganged are ideal for most presentations. If the baits are being attacked by bream rather than tailor, change to a four hook gang of 3/0's to give more chance on the smaller mouthed bream.

On snapper we prefer just a two hook gang as this allows for presentation of half pilchards which seem very attractive to smaller snapper.

The key to successful pilchard presentations on ganged hooks is to ensure that the hook closest to the angler goes through the eye of the pilchard. The eye socket and skull are the only strong part of the fish and the rig works by using this as the anchor point for the bait.

When baiting up the gang with a pilchard, lay the gang along the bait and have the bottom part of the leading hook sitting right over the middle of the pilchard's eye. Use your thumb and forefinger to press the bottom end of the trailing hook firmly against the fish. This mark will be the place where you start putting the point of the hook, then the next hook, ending with the leading hook being accurately positioned through the eye of the pilchard.

When using pilchards on gangs it is vital that the bait lay straight and natural and not curve around as this causes the bait to spin in the water and look quite unnatural to the fish.

While whole pilchards work well, plenty of fish are taken using pilchard pieces. The best parts for bait being the head and tail sections. These are usually rigged by putting the whole hook through either the eye or narrow part of the tail and then positioning the hook in the bait.

The eye of the hook provides a large surface that does not generally pull back through the bait.

The centre body portion of the pilchard can be chopped into pieces for berley or kept in case needed as bait when the heads and tails run out.

The best hooks for rigging pilchard pieces are Suicide and Viking patterns.

Above: Head section of pilchard.
Below: Pilchards fished on ganged hooks are top baits for a wide variety of fish.

IQF pilchards in packet and block pilchards.

normally an added extra and should not be relied on as a source of bait.

A few boats also net pilchards on the east coast for the fresh fish markets in Sydney and Melbourne. While these pilchards are sometimes in good shape, they are rarely as good as the frozen commercial product from Western Australia.

Handling

While most pilchards are in very good condition when purchased it always pays to check them carefully before you buy. Top quality pilchards have bright blue backs and a sharp silvery shine on the body. The eyes should be clear and black. Check the belly area carefully for any discolouration or ruptures.

It doesn't take long to become a good judge of a pilchard. Pilchards in poor condition go soft very quickly and are nearly useless as bait when this happens.

While IQF (Individually Quick Frozen) pilchards produce few usage problems there are plenty of times when a whole block of pilchards is just too much for one outing.

The trick here is to drop the block onto a flat, hard surface. This fractures the block usually close to half and half while it is still frozen with no damage to the baits. You can use one half and put the other half back in the freezer.

It is not uncommon to finish a fishing session with plenty of thawed but unused

pilchards. The baits can be refrozen and used as berley next time out, and they do make great berley. Or the baits can be salted and reused next time out.

The way to salt pilchards is as follows. Put down a layer of course salt on some newspaper, lay the pilchards flat on the salt and then cover with more salt. Cover the whole lot with more newspaper and place on a flat tray in the fridge.

Leave in the salt for 24 hours and then remove. Dust off the salt and then place in a plastic bag in the freezer. The salted pilchards may not be as bright and shiny as fresh ones but they are much tougher and most fish will still take them.

Points of Note

The bait suppliers and processors actually produce three products.

IQF pilchards are as the initials indicate, individually quick frozen. They come in cartons of 2 and 5 kg and are repacked by bait shops and bait processors in half or one kilo bags. These separated, well packaged baits are very useful when only a small quantity of pilchards is needed.

Block pilchards are 2 kg packs with all the fish frozen together. The block occurs because the fish are wet when they are packed into the trays which give the product its characteristic shape.

Twenty kilogram blocks of second grade pilchards are produced for the commercial fishing market. These are used as trap and craypot bait but yellowfin and mackerel anglers also use these blocks as an important source of cheap berley. These blocks sell for half the price of comparable first grade pilchards.

There are few better baits than the pilchard, it has universal appeal to a wide spread of fish. It is used in the estuary, off the rocks and beaches and at sea. It is one of the great 'all round' baits.

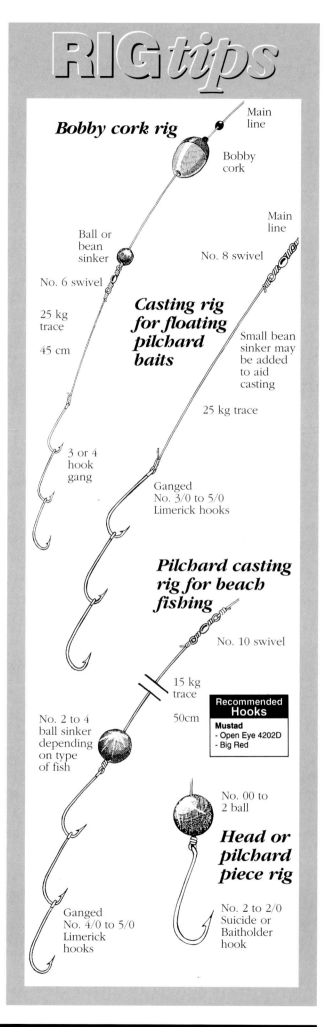

Prawns

Prawns are one of the most popular and commonly used baits available to anglers.

They can be caught in many places and used live, or they can be purchased fresh or frozen from bait shops.

The prawn itself is a large member of the shrimp family and a wide range of species are available around the country, however most bait prawns belong to the *Penaeid* group.

Prawns are found in estuaries and offshore and are an important food source for a wide variety of fish and an important commercial product for the fishing industry.

For most anglers prawns come from a bait supply, but the very best prawns, live ones, are usually caught by the angler, kept alive and then used as bait.

Live prawns are one of the best baits available particularly for estuary anglers.

Where to Find Them

The prawns most anglers have access to are found in the estuaries and in tropical areas along sheltered beaches near the mouth of rivers and creeks. Sandflats with fringing weed beds are always likely spots.

In the tropics prawns are regularly caught in cast nets, by working the edges of deep holes, small gutters and in the channels on the edges of many beaches. Sometimes the prawns are in high concentrations but mostly there is just enough for bait which is the aim of the exercise.

Most prawn grounds in any area are well known and local tackle shops should be able to advise anglers of the best spots to try.

Some lakes have distinct 'runs' when the prawns migrate to sea and good catches are made by scoop netting the prawns with the aid of a lantern or strong torch.

Prawns are most active during the new moon or dark phase of the moon each month. They are available for most of the year but are easiest to find during the warmer months.

How to Catch Them

In temperate zones, the prawns can be caught with either drag nets or scoop nets and bright lights.

Working a prawn drag net or bait net in the tropics is just a matter of dragging the net along for about 15 or 20 minutes and then beach-

Prawning on a hot summers night is lots of fun.

How to Use Them

The key to using prawns is to present them so they are attractive to the fish. The most important thing is to keep the prawn straight when placed on the hook. This is regardless of whether you are using the prawn alive, dead, peeled or unpeeled. The key is to always thread the prawn onto the hook from the tail, not trying to fit too much of the prawn onto the hook. Hooks with bait holding slices on the shank help keep the prawn in a natural position.

With live prawns the hook can be passed through the body from the side near the tail or secondly, passed through the first two or three segments before emerging. This later method also works well with fresh or frozen prawns.

No matter what method of baiting is used, it is important to ensure the prawn is not curled around the hook. Educated fish know this is a fake and avoid it easily. However the same fish will readily attack a live or well presented fresh prawn.

Right top: Rigged live prawn ideal for casting and drifting.
Right: Prawns hooked through one segment of the tail make for an ideal live bait presentation.
Below: Eastern king prawn.

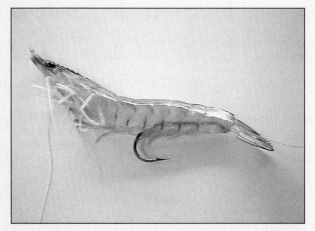

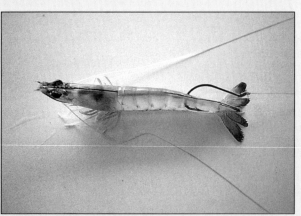

Matthew Yalouris with a good catch of prawns taken with a scoop net and a strong torch.

ing it and sorting the catch.

The advantage of drag and bait nets is the range of other baits that they capture. Small fish like mullet, hardi-heads, glassies, garfish and herring all turn up in the net along with squid, crabs and other shrimps.

The use of a scoop net also allows the capture of a few extra bits and pieces particularly squid and small fish which are attracted to the light.

Prawns are usually spotted by the red reflection of their eyes and their distinctive shape. They are then scooped into the net and shaken down into the pocket.

Often when they are found feeding on the bottom they are best netted using two people and two scoops to force them into one net or the other. The prawns often swim along the surface which makes them easy to net.

The one real advantage of the scoop net is the small size of its mesh. This enables it to catch and hold much smaller size prawns than a drag net. As a bait, small prawns are excellent,

and size is only relevant if the prawns are to be eaten.

Handling

Prawns catch more fish if kept alive. The best way to do this is in seawater with an aerator, or for short periods, in wet seaweed or rolled in a wet sugar bag. Most importantly, they need to be kept at a constant temperature. Use an ice box or cooler of some kind and keep it in a shady spot. Once out fishing, freshen the prawns with regular changes of seawater. Always remember to handle the prawns carefully during capture and holding. Like all shellfish they can be easily damaged by careless handling.

If the prawns are thick and you catch more than you require for bait, the obvious thing is to eat the excess. However, they can also be preserved for future use as bait by freezing them in salty water.

Use a take-away food container, filled three quarters full of prawns, cover them with salty water and put the lid on and freeze. When they thaw out they will still look fresh and green and make excellent bait

Points of Note

Fresh prawns and packaged frozen prawns tend to be highly variable in quality and care needs to be taken when purchasing them for bait. Always look for good green colour, and no black colouration around the head, shell or legs.

If the prawns look dry and broken, they may also be second rate. Look at them as they thaw and remember what good ones and bad ones looked like.

When buying prawns, always check the product carefully because the fish will when the same bait is on the end of the hook.

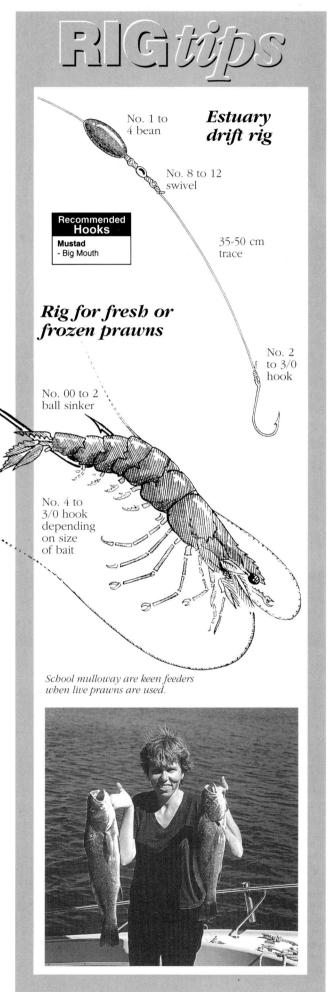

Estuary drift rig

No. 1 to 4 bean

No. 8 to 12 swivel

Recommended Hooks
Mustad - Big Mouth

35-50 cm trace

No. 2 to 3/0 hook

Rig for fresh or frozen prawns

No. 00 to 2 ball sinker

No. 4 to 3/0 hook depending on size of bait

School mulloway are keen feeders when live prawns are used.

Razor*fish*

Razorfish *(Pinna menkei)* are a large bivalve that inhabit the estuaries of south-east Australia. Razorfish are gathered both as bait and for human consumption although the yield of meat from these very large shellfish is fairly small, with the useable meat area only as big as a twenty cent piece.

The razorfish gets its name from the way it buries vertically in the mud leaving only its sharp, flaky edge level with the surface of the mud. Many people wandering shoe-less in the shallows have found out painfully how the razorfish gets its name.

Most estuary fish will eat razorfish with fish like King George whiting, leatherjackets, bream, trevally, wrasse and parrot fish all keen to eat these shellfish.

Razorfish are not available commercially and need to be harvested by the angler. Often a few are picked up as part of other bait gathering activities but razorfish can be found in numbers in some areas and are easily harvested.

Where to Find Them

While razorfish are common in many estuaries in south eastern Australia, they are not as popular a bait in New South Wales compared to Victoria and South Australia where they are keenly harvested. The main reason for this is the presence of King George whiting in these two states and razorfish being one of the best baits to target this species.

Razorfish are collected from the deep edges of mud banks at low tide, although the greatest populations are found just a little deeper in 2 to 3 metres of water just off the end of the mudflats.

How to Catch Them

Razorfish when found on

How to Use Them

The razorfish has a hard section know as the heart and a soft gut section that is attached around the heart. Being firm it is the heart that is most important for bait as this part will hold a hook quite well.

The actual amount of bait in each shell is quite small, but the heart can be cut into three or four baits to economise and use of the bait for best results.

Bait size used will depend on the fish being sought as much as anything. On whiting, the bait can be cut into three or four pieces to suit the No.4 size hooks commonly used.

On bream only two baits may be available to fit the No.2 to 1/0 size hooks used. On fish like sweep and leatherjackets a No.6 hook works well. Best hook patterns are Baitholders, Suicide, Eastern Estuary and Long Shank.

Razor fish are a bivalve mollusc like a mussel or cockle only a good deal larger.

Shrimp *pistol*

Pistol shrimp also known as green nippers are so named for the sharp cracking sound they make both when captured and while feeding underwater. The sound is made by the very distinctive large claw of these shrimp which can also painfully nip the unwary bait gatherer.

Pistol shrimp can be found right around Australia, both in the estuaries and on the ocean rocks.

As a bait it has wide appeal but it is often overlooked by anglers. The main reason for the lack of interest is the difficulty in obtaining big numbers of the bait and its comparatively small size, growing to about 8 cm in length but being more common at about 5 cm.

By learning how to harvest and use this bait, anglers can add substantially to their captures.

The green nipper is a very popular bait with whiting, bream, trevally, flounder, flathead and school mulloway.

Where to Find Them

Green nippers are a creature of the estuary foreshores although a very closely related species is found in ocean rock pools. They are usually found under rocks, timber or other shelter which is close to the intertidal limit.

As a rule they prefer the rocks or timber that holds some residual water under them during low tide. On the ocean rocks they are found under rocks and stones within tidal pools, usually in the shallow parts where rocks, sand and mud are mixed.

They are also a very common shrimp around seagrass beds and any rock or timber lying within a seagrass bed will almost always yield a pair of green nippers when turned over.

How to Catch Them

Because these shrimps live under some form of cover, the way to catch them is to turn over the rocks or timber lying on the mud of the intertidal zones.

Once the rock or timber is turned over look carefully particularly in any small pools of water now left under the exposed shelter area. The pistol shrimp can be hard to see at times, but a well trained eye will quickly spot them.

They are usually found in pairs and are picked up and dropped into a bucket partially filled with seawater. Replace the rock so it continues to provide a shelter for other inhabitants.

This turning over of rocks for bait will yield all sorts of useable goodies. Small crabs are common, a few prawns turn up and quite a few blood worms and wriggler worms can also be grabbed.

It is important to note this form of bait gathering is legal in many areas like

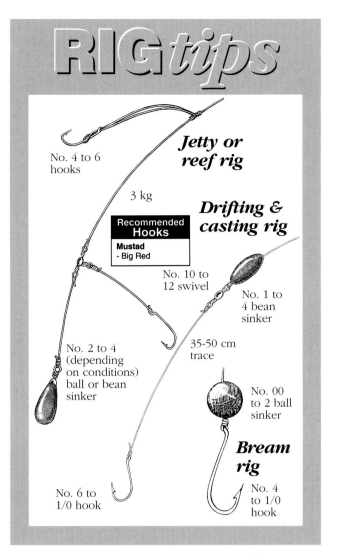

Jetty or reef rig

No. 4 to 6 hooks

3 kg

Recommended **Hooks**

Mustad - Big Red

No. 10 to 12 swivel

No. 2 to 4 (depending on conditions) ball or bean sinker

No. 6 to 1/0 hook

Drifting & casting rig

No. 1 to 4 bean sinker

35-50 cm trace

No. 00 to 2 ball sinker

Bream rig

No. 4 to 1/0 hook

the mudflats can be pulled fairly easily from the ground. The trick is to spot them as they are often well camouflaged but sometimes their presence is made obvious by walking on them with a shoe.

In the deeper water, the razorfish tend to be only half buried in the mud and a substantial part of their shell remains exposed. While more easily seen, accessing them is more difficult.

Most of the gathering of razorfish in deeper water is done with wooden tongs about 3 or 4 metres long. These tongs have a lever operated arm that grabs the razorfish and holds it all the way to the boat. This operation needs clear water and calm conditions to work properly. The tongs are available in tackle shops in South Australia and Victoria.

Handling

Like most shellfish from the intertidal zone, razorfish are hardy and will stay alive for

several days if kept in a cool spot. This can be assisted by a daily dunking in fresh seawater. Generally though, the meat is removed from the shell and used fresh or frozen.

Razorfish freeze very well and thaw out in excellent shape. To freeze this bait for any length of time it is necessary to remove the meat and place it in a container and cover it with seawater before sealing it.

Points of Note

The warning about wearing shoes on mudflats is important and not just because of razorfish.

While razorfish may cause a bad cut in areas where they are common, sadly these days broken glass and used hypodermics can also turn up.

The days of being barefoot and carefree in our beautiful estuaries are gone. Shoes always made sense anyway, but they are even more important now.

Sydney Harbour where bait digging is officially prohibited.

Handling

Pistol shrimp are fairly hardy creatures and can live in either wet seaweed or in a container of seawater with an aerator. As with all live sea creatures it is important to store them in a cool, shady place if keeping them for use the next day.

Points of Note

If using pistol shrimp as bait in rocky areas for bream, be aware that the shrimp will instinctively seek shelter under rocks once it hits the bottom.

This can lead to continual snagging in some areas. The

How to Use Them

Putting a pistol shrimp on the hook needs attention to detail and the use of small, fine hooks. Being a smallish bait to start with hooks need to match the physical dimensions of the bait. The best hooks are No.6 to No.4 in Long Shank type patterns, although some anglers may prefer a fine gauge Suicide type if looking for bream and trevally. The aim of the small, fine hook is to present the bait alive and in an attractive manner to the fish.

The hook is inserted under the tail flap and the bait is curled around the bend of the hook. Bring the point of the hook out of the body well along the tail section near where it joins the head section. The size of the shrimp will dictate how much of the tail section will go on the hook. Quality fish will take a live pistol shrimp whole and without hesitation including the hook. It is more important to present the bait alive and attractively than try to get too much bait on the hook.

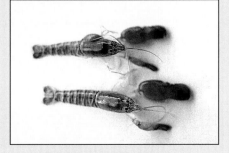

Above: Pistol shrimp rigged on a hook.
Right: Profile of pistol shrimps.

See Estuary Shrimps for Pistol Shrimp rig tips.

trick is to use the shrimp over sand areas or keep it off the bottom by using a

float rig or paternoster rig if fishing over rocks. Using the bait while drifting from a

boat will also avoid such problems and give the shrimp no chance to snag.

Shrimp *estuary*

Despite its small size, approximately 2.5 cm, the shrimp is a plentiful, easily caught bait that catches a lot of fish when used correctly.

The shrimp has only a few followers in more northern areas but in southern waters it is used extensively on bream, whiting, flounder, trevally and flathead.

Whiting anglers in particular use this little shrimp when other baits like worms or yabbies are hard to come by or just to save money on more expensive baits.

The shrimp itself is a major part of the estuary food chain and many varieties of fish spend much of their feeding time stalking these small, agile and aggressive crustaceans.

The shrimp is a scavenger, eagerly clouding onto any fish frame or dead fish and rapidly reducing it to a skeleton. This is its job in nature and for anglers who look carefully at their environment once these shrimp are identified it is amazing how common they are.

Where to Find Them

There are lots of different estuary shrimp but the main specie is the humpy back *(Hippolyte spp.)* which lives in or near weed beds and around any area with a bit of weedy cover or where fish frames and other offal regularly enters the water.

Ribbon weed beds are by far the most reliable areas to catch viable quantities for bait. They are also easiest to catch in these areas.

How to Catch Them

The ribbon weed is used by the shrimp as both a place to shelter and a place to feed. They are caught by using a fine gauge scoop net or a prawn net with a large fist size ball of dead ribbon weed placed in the end of the net.

The net is then driven along the bottom of the ribbon weed, against the current if there is any, for three or four metres and the contents in the end are then sorted. The larger shrimp are kept for bait and everything else is returned to the water.

Working this way it is often possible to catch 100

Bream are regularly caught using shrimp as bait.

How to Use Them

Being very small baits, shrimp need matching small hooks to maintain good presentation. This also means unintentionally catching quite a few undersized fish at times. Some of the fine gauge, chemically sharpened hooks provide plenty of options when using shrimp. Sizes around No.6 or No.8 are about perfect for shrimp fishing.

The baits are put on by passing the hook under the tail of the shrimp and then bending the shrimp gently to follow the curve of the hook and bringing it out among the legs area about half way along the tail.

Another good rig is to put two shrimp on the hook, set back to back so they flick and click against one another. This movement often attracts the interest of any fish in the area.

Shrimp fishing is best suited to working with light tackle and fine presentations. Most shrimp are fished by anglers using light tackle for estuary fish. The best rig for most situations is to set the hook on a 35 to 50 cm trace joined to a swivel with a small running sinker. These baits also work well under lightweight float rigs.

Shrimp rigged on light gauge hook.

Collecting shrimp in weed beds with fine mesh nets.

baits in a very short period of time. Only take as many baits as needed.

An alternative to using the dip net is to use a folding shrimp trap, preferably the fine gauge type, baited with some fish or meat. These traps are available at most tackle shops.

These little bait traps will catch plenty of shrimp if left in the weed beds overnight. The shrimp traps will also work under jetties and other spots where shrimp often gather.

Handling

Shrimp are hardy creatures and will survive quite long periods in captivity although they are prone to eat each other if kept confined together for too long.

They need either regular changes of water or a small air pump to maintain the oxygen level in the container. A small cooler is also handy because of its high surface area for oxygen absorption and its capacity to maintain stable water temperature.

Store the container in a cool, shady spot. High temperatures kill baits faster than anything else. Always check the bucket or container and remove any dead shrimp as this will also contaminate the water.

Shrimp and small fish collected in net.

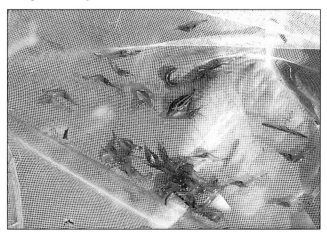

Shrimp rig for lightweight presentation

Estuary shrimp
No. 10 to 6 hook

Pistol shrimp
No. 6 to 2 hook

No. 0 to 2 ball sinker

No. 1 to 3 bug or bean sinker

Recommended Hooks
Mustad
- Baitholder 92247
- Red Baitholder

35-50 cm trace

Casting & drifting rig for shrimp

Estuary shrimp
No. 10 to 6 hook

Pistol shrimp
No. 6 to 2 hook

Silver trevally are keen feeders on shrimp.

Shrimp *freshwater*

Silver perch are keen shrimp feeders.

Almost all freshwater systems around the country have a population of shrimp of some kind. They vary in size from tiny 2 to 3 cm models through to the large 12 cm Murray river shrimp which is as big as a prawn. Freshwater shrimp are an important bait particularly for bass and impoundment anglers looking for silver perch, yellowbelly and small cod.

Where to Find Them

The best place to find shrimp is always around some form of natural cover. Weed beds, dense snags, fallen trees, heavy in-water bankside vegetation or similar structures are all home to the shrimp.

How to Catch Them

By far the easiest method of catching shrimp is to use a collapsible shrimp trap available at most tackle stores. These clever little traps have taken all the hard work out of catching shrimps, crayfish and minnows.

The trap is weighted with a small river stone and baited with meat, fish or whatever the local fad happens to be. On the Murray, raw, frozen dim sims from the freezer chest at the local supermarket are very popular but it depends on what is available.

The trap is set in the weed beds or beside a snag or whatever with the funnels of the trap facing directly up and down current. If the trap is layed across the current nothing will enter the funnels. The trap is usually set overnight but it will catch during the day and can be checked every couple of hours if necessary.

Shrimp can also be caught by running a fine gauge net through weed beds always working into the current to ensure any dislodged shrimp finish in the net.

Handling

Shrimp are best kept in a container of aerated water,

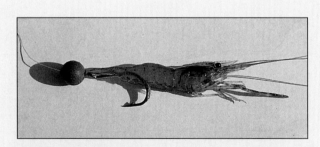

How to Use Them

In most situations the best presentation is two shrimp on one hook fished back to back. Fished in this way the shrimp tend to struggle and flick as they make contact and this draws any nearby fish to investigate.

Larger shrimp can be fished on a single hook with good results, particularly on bass.

The most important part of the presentation is to use a hook size to match the size of the shrimp available. Small, fine gauge hooks work best, this may also mean playing the fish gently when hooked.

On very small shrimp, hooks from No.8 to No.12 may be used, particularly on trout. On more average size shrimp hooks from No.6 to No.2 are used.

The best rigs for using shrimp tend to be float rigs on trout and bass allowing the bait to be set in open water and drifted past where a fish is likely to be feeding.

On native fish, a small sinker running right to the hook or a paternoster rig are the best choice. These rigs allow the bait to be fished right in the snags and the baits can be gently raised and lowered to add struggle and appeal to the bait.

By placing the hook in the tail of the shrimp it will remain alive and attractive to the fish for a long time.

Bottom fishing rig

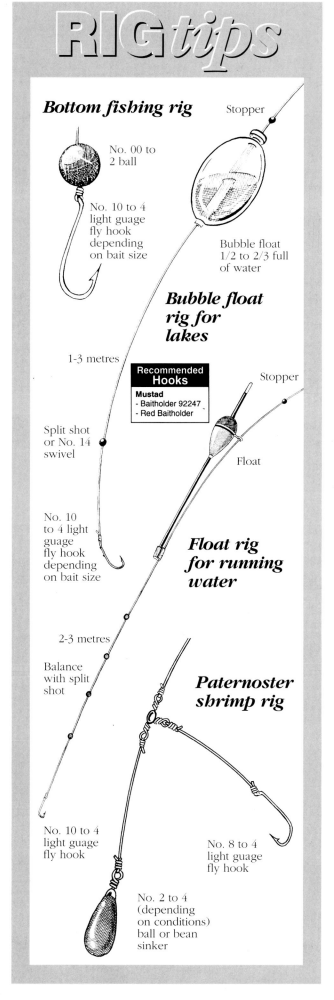

Stopper

No. 00 to 2 ball

No. 10 to 4 light guage fly hook depending on bait size

Bubble float 1/2 to 2/3 full of water

Bubble float rig for lakes

1-3 metres

Recommended Hooks
Mustad
- Baitholder 92247
- Red Baitholder

Stopper

Float

Split shot or No. 14 swivel

No. 10 to 4 light guage fly hook depending on bait size

Float rig for running water

2-3 metres

Balance with split shot

Paternoster shrimp rig

No. 10 to 4 light guage fly hook

No. 8 to 4 light guage fly hook

No. 2 to 4 (depending on conditions) ball or bean sinker

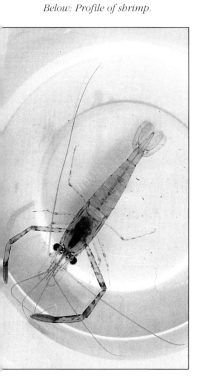

Above: Collecting freshwater shrimp in weed beds using a fine gauge net.
Below: Profile of shrimp.

something like a small esky is ideal. They will also stay alive if stored in wet river weed or rolled in a wet hessian sack.

The container is then stored in a cool, shady spot.

The key to fishing with shrimp is to use them live, they seem fairly unattractive to the fish when dead.

Points of Note

One trick when using freshwater shrimp is to place two shrimp on the one hook set back to back.

This arrangement tends to make the shrimp struggle and kick which is highly attractive to any fish hunting in the area.

Just pass the hook once through one body segment and then thread on another shrimp so they end up back to back.

Squid

Fresh squid are always good bait for ocean fish.

Squid belong to the same class of animals as the octopus, nautilus and cuttlefish, that of the Cephalopoda. The name means head-footed for in these animals the foot, which is divided up into a number of arms is wrapped around the head.

Squid are a common capture in both estuary and offshore waters and they make great bait. As a bait, they are also readily available in frozen form and fresh through bait and sea-food outlets. In years gone by, squid were a very cheap bait but cultural changes in Australia have made squid a popular table and restaurant species which means they now cost more.

Anglers catch squid for the table as well as for bait. The exercise of catching squid is much like that of catching prawns, where the bait is as attractive food to the anglers as it is to the fish. Still you can always eat the bait which is what often happens when squid fishing.

Where to Find Them

Squid like fairly salty water and do not move very far upstream in coastal rivers but they are particularly common in deep estuaries and harbours. They are also attracted by lights at night and can often be found around bridges and wharf areas which are well lit.

Offshore, they regularly turn up around headlands, over kelp beds, around bait grounds and on offshore reefs. Sometimes they can be a real pest when live baiting as they attack baits intended for bigger fish.

Squid are very aggressive hunters eating small fish and prawns. That's why squid are common wherever bait fish are common.

How to Catch Them

There are a range of ways to catch squid, most of them rely on some form of multi-prong hook that will find its way onto the tentacles of an attacking squid.

The introduction of prawn-shaped keeled lures from Asia has lead to a revolution in squid fishing. These lures are extremely attractive to the squid which attack them greedily only to find themselves caught by the multi-pronged hook on the end of the lure.

These prawn type lures are usually fished from a light spinning rod, with the lure cast out and allowed to sink. It is then twitched and pulsed slowly back to the boat. Alternatively the lure can be set 2 metres under a bobby float and cast out.

The movement of the bobby float gives action to the lure below and when it is grabbed by the squid it almost always hooks up. It is then a simple matter of winding in the squid. This

Imitation prawn squid jigs are by far the best method of catching squid.

How to Use Them

Small squid when used whole are rigged with either a single hook in the top of the body tube or by using two linked hooks to hook both the top of the tube with one hook and the head with the other.

Often, small squid heads are used whole and the tube is cut into strips. Squid heads are always good bait. The only thing to ensure is that the size of the bait suits the size of the fish available. Hook sizes depend on the size

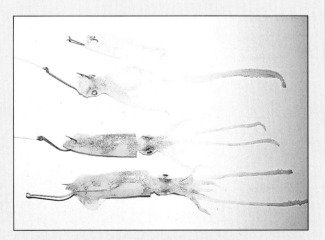

of the bait and the type of fish being sought.

Larger squid are usually cut into bait sized strips, and with really large specimens each tentacle becomes a bait.

Squid is a tough bait and it stays on the hook as well as anything that is available. It also stays in good shape when attacked by pickers which can be handy in many locations.

Whole squid and squid pieces rigged for bait.

Nathan Falla with a squid caught spinning with prawn jigs from the rocks near Sydney.

technique is extremely effective off the ocean rocks.

Other squid catching systems rely on a real bait fish such as a pilchard or yellowtail. These are set on a spike or piece of metal rod with a set of hooks all around the bottom which act as a jag.

The bait is placed head down on the metal rod so it is closest to the prongs. The reason for this is that squid tend to attack the head of the bait and locating it closest to the hooks provides the best chance of driving the prongs into the squid.

Squid are also caught in prawn nets as a by catch. They can be scoop netted or speared around bridges and wharves. Sometimes they attack a bait intended for other fish and hang on long enough to be led into a waiting landing net.

Handling

All squid can squirt a black ink-like substance, it's part of their defence system. Knowing this, it pays to drop the squid straight into a bucket or cooler immediately on capture.

Squid do not stay alive very long in a bait tank al-

though they can be hooked up at the point of capture and dropped straight back over the side. Rigged this way, live squid are an enticing bait for mulloway, snapper and fingermark bream.

The flesh of squid is affected by contact with freshwater, changing it from clear or opaque to white. While this does not have much impact on its use as bait, the squid looks a lot better if stored in a plastic bag with ice around the plastic bag rather than placing the squid directly on ice. Often, seawater is placed in a bag or bucket and ice is packed around it.

Whichever way you do it, squid need careful handling after capture to keep them looking good for use as bait or on the table.

Points of Note

If buying squid for bait always look for good colour and check that the surface skin, which is covered in very fine dots, is still intact. Squid in poor condition look watery, have a white or off-white colour and the outer layer of skin breaks up quite clearly.

Some squid offered for both bait and food is of average quality so always check before purchase.

The same goes for packaged frozen squid. Have a good look at what is in the packet before paying for it.

Squid are top bait for fingermark bream.

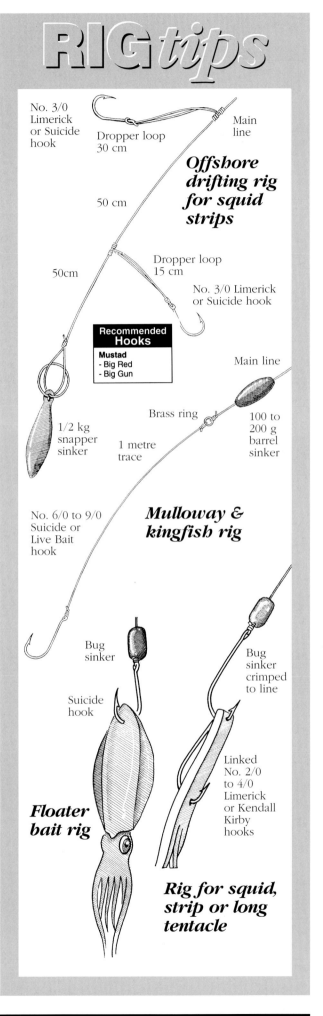

No. 3/0 Limerick or Suicide hook

Dropper loop 30 cm

Main line

Offshore drifting rig for squid strips

50 cm

50cm

Dropper loop 15 cm

No. 3/0 Limerick or Suicide hook

Main line

Recommended Hooks
Mustad
- Big Red
- Big Gun

Brass ring

100 to 200 g barrel sinker

1/2 kg snapper sinker

1 metre trace

No. 6/0 to 9/0 Suicide or Live Bait hook

Mulloway & kingfish rig

Bug sinker

Suicide hook

Bug sinker crimped to line

Linked No. 2/0 to 4/0 Limerick or Kendall Kirby hooks

Floater bait rig

Rig for squid, strip or long tentacle

Tuna *small*

Small tuna species are both fun to catch and are an important bait fish for bottom anglers and game and sport fishermen. These tuna are used as strip baits, live baits, troll and whole dead baits.

Different species turn up around the country but in most cases it is fish like bonito, frigate mackerel, striped tuna, mackerel tuna and longtail tuna that make up the bulk of the catches.

It matters little what the species is or where it is found as there are a couple of basic tactics and techniques that will catch these valuable bait fish wherever they are encountered.

Having access to really fresh or live oceanic baits can be a vital part of catching offshore fish. In some cases it can be the difference between catching a big fish or missing out completely.

Bottom anglers benefit too by having premium strip baits available to catch their favourite fish. Nothing beats a fresh, juicy strip of tuna or bonito. Fresh cut baits also hold together much better than pieces of frozen bait.

Where to Find Them

Small tuna are found around offshore reefs, islands, bommies or schooling in the open ocean. They are predominantly a school fish and can often be caught in big numbers.

At these times anglers can selectively catch the fish and freeze or salt them for later use. Either way it will yield big savings on bait purchases later. These appearances by the fish may be seasonal and well known, so planning to harvest them is often part of the fishing program.

In the open sea the tuna are often visible feeding on the surface with flocks of birds wheeling around them. Closer to shore current lines and the edges of offshore formations are always likely.

Many of the fish are caught by having the right sort of lures out while travelling to and from the fishing grounds.

How to Catch Them

There are two basic methods of capture, trolling and lure casting.

The best trolling lures are very small metal or plastic headed lures with squid or tinsel skirts attached. Small feather lures are also very good. The best colours are pink, white, red, purple or combinations with tinsel added.

The lures are rigged with Limerick or Tarpon style hooks on about two metres of 30 to 40 kg nylon trace. The trace is used to swing the fish aboard to avoid wasting time netting or gaffing the fish.

The lures are set 15 to 20 metres behind the boat and trolled at a speed of 5 to 8 knots. Reels loaded with 6 to 10 kg line are best for this

Snapper are regularly caught using strips of fresh small tuna as bait.

type of work. When a school of fish is located the boat circles the outside of the school until hook-ups occur. The fish are retrieved and the process starts again.

A quicker method of hauling in the bait is to use troll lines which are 15 metres of venetian blind cord linked by a strong swivel to 4 me-

How to Use Them

Small tuna and bonito have two basic rolls as bait fish. For anglers seeking table fish they are a source of prime strip baits. For anglers seeking game and sports fish they are used as live bait or dead baits rigged using a variety of methods.

Far right: Bonito cut into strip baits. Right: Fillet of small tuna with strip baits. Below: Strip baits ready for use.

Game and sport fishing anglers often bridle these baits using a piece of 10 to 15 kg dacron and a bait needle. These bridled live baits are then slowly trolled around likely areas looking for marlin or big yellowfin tuna.

Rigged as dead baits these small tuna present a wide range of options. They can be made to skip or swim for trolling or set as drift baits or used as shark baits.

Small tuna are an important offshore bait fish and knowing how to catch them makes sure this bait supply is available both fresh and frozen.

tres of 50 to 70 kg nylon trace. The lure remains the same but is fitted with a 3/0 or 4/0, extra strong treble hook or a 6/0 or 8/0 Tarpon hook. The technique is brutal but fast and has the bait in the boat quickly.

Casting metal lures on threadline or overhead reels at schools of feeding fish is also very effective.

Lures that can be worked at fast retrieve speeds without spinning or twisting are best. Small chromed leadfish or cut metal rod type lures are the most popular types.

Rig the lures on a 50 cm trace of 25 kg nylon line linked by a small swivel.

It is important that the reels used in this type of fishing have a high gear ratio so the lures can be retrieved at a speed attractive to the fish.

Handling

Anglers seeking surface fish for same day use as bait are best advised to drop the baits straight onto ice. This 'sets' the flesh and keeps it in perfect condition until needed.

If the bait is really thick and the boat has gone to sea just to catch a heap of bait for future use then a bin of ice slurry is required. This is a mixture of seawater and ice, starting off with one third seawater and two thirds ice but growing as the ice melts as the warm fish enter the mixture.

Ice slurried fish cool quickly and are in ideal condition when frozen for later use.

Small tuna, bonito and frigate mackerel will not survive very long in most live bait tanks, although they will last a couple of minutes while the boat charges over to the chosen fishing location from the spots where they were hooked. Bonito last the best and frigate mackerel the worst when placed in a bait tank.

Small tuna and bonito can be salted and preserved for later use. The salting process toughens the bait but it remains extremely attractive to the fish.

The fish are prepared by filleting them and coating the whole fillet in coarse butchers salt. The flesh side of the fillet has the salt firmly but gently rubbed into the flesh.

The salt coated fillets are placed on a bed of newspaper with a bit of extra salt coating over the top. Several layers of newspaper salted fillet and salt can be placed in one container if necessary.

After 24 hours the fillets are removed from the salt and any excess salt dusted off. The fillets are then placed in plastic bags and consigned to the freezer.

When thawed, these baits will be just as good as the fresh article and they do catch plenty of fish.

Points of Note

Plenty of ice is essential when catching small tuna for bait. Using bulk ice suppliers can save lots of money compared to conventional purchases of party ice from local garages.

Places like fish markets, fish co-operatives and ice manufacturers supply bulk ice at very cheap prices. By having plenty of ice a big catch of bait can be properly handled and kept in top shape until ready to prepare for the freezer.

Small bonito caught on a bait jig is dropped into the bait tank.

RIGtips

Rig for floating strip baits

Brass ring or small swivel

No. 1 to 3 bean

35-50 cm

Main line

Solid brass ring

No. 1/0 to 6/0 hook

Solid brass ring

45-60 cm

Snapper rig for tuna strip

30-40 cm

60 to 120 g snapper sinker

No. 2/0 to 8/0 hook

No. 3/0 hook

Main line

Dropper loop 30 cm

50 cm

Offshore drifting rig

Dropper loop 15 cm

Main line

50 cm

No. 3/0 hook

Brass ring

100 to 200 g barrel sinker

Mulloway & kingfish rig

1 metre trace

Recommended **Hooks**
Mustad - Big Red

No. 6/0 to 9/0 hook

Cabbage (*Ulva lactuca*) is a seaweed used to catch luderick and rock blackfish. It is a form of sea lettuce and is actually edible by man as well as the

Cabbage is usually gathered on the ocean rocks at low tide.

fish. While many Australians are only recent converts to the taste sensations of seaweed via Japanese sushi, seaweeds have been a dietary item on the menu of many cultures for centuries.

However, most Australians don't eat raw cabbage, but fish do and it is an important bait for both rock and estuary anglers.

Where to Find It

Cabbage is found on rock shelves and in rock pools in the ocean intertidal zone. In favourable areas it forms considerable 'gardens' of sea lettuce, often on walls or ledges which are constantly washed by the sea or on sloping rocks that are submerged for most of each tidal cycle.

It grows in leafy clumps and is easily distinguished from all other seaweeds by both its shape and the way it secures itself to the rocks, sprouting leafy fronds which build up in a concentric pattern. It is in shape and form just like its land based name sake cabbage, although it has no firm tissue like a land cabbage.

Collecting Cabbage

The weed is generally easy to collect on rock shelves. Most anglers fishing on rock platforms tend to just collect it and use it as they go along but it may depend on where the angler wants to fish. At times the cabbage may need to be collected and transported to another location.

Cabbage forms distinctive rosettes on the rocks and is easily gathered for bait.

Cabbage is also good for catching estuary luderick and many anglers harvest cabbage on the ocean rocks for later use in the estuary. Cabbage is excellent bait for luderick along the rockwalls that line the entrance to so many of the rivers along the east coast.

To collect the cabbage,

How to Use Cabbage

On the ocean rocks, the cabbage is used just as it is found. Usually a leaf or little cluster of leaves is put on the hook and a half hitch is placed around the top of the hook to hold everything in position and maintain the shape of the cabbage in the water.

For luderick, usually one leaf at a time is used. For rock blackfish (drummer) the whole cluster can be used. Again a half hitch is used to keep the cluster on the hook and maintain its shape. Hooks for luderick are No.8 to No.6 and No.2 to 2/0 for rock blackfish.

In the estuary, just one leaf at a time is used, usually a small portion looped on to look like a small rosette. Some very successful exponents using cabbage in the estuaries fold the cabbage leaves into a series of quarters almost like folding pieces of paper into little squares about as big as a finger nail. These 'folds' of leaf are then hooked once straight through one corner, from side to side in the area of tightest folding. This bait then makes a little fan shape in the water which the fish seem to find highly attractive. Hook sizes for estuary luderick are usually No.10 to No.6 depending on the size of the fish in the area.

Green weed and baited hook.

How to Use Green Weed

Putting weed onto a hook has always been one of the great skills of the keen luderick angler. The key is to not use too much weed. Just tease out a dozen or so strands and then roll them into a thin string using the thumb working across the middle finger and forefinger. This rolling binds the strands together so they stay firmly on the hook and allows the weed to be easily laid onto the hook. To put the weed on the hook, fold the now stringy weed in the middle at the top of the hook then overlay the weed in a cris cross pattern down the shank of the hook. This should look like a two strand plait and sit firmly on the hook.

Leave a long, juicy end about 2.5 to 3 cm below the hook to allow the luderick to taste the bait before taking the hook. The key is to make the bait slim and easy for the fish to eat and swallow. Luderick tend to play around with baits that they cannot easily draw into their mouths.

The best hook patterns for luderick are Eastern Estuary (green), Sneck and Suicide.

Cabbage bait needs a half hitch at the top of the hook.

Hook baited with green weed.

just pinch it off at the base and put it in a plastic bait bucket or whatever holding system is available. Only take as much cabbage as is needed for the fishing at hand. Don't over harvest the bait supply, its also an important food item for the local fish population.

Handling Cabbage

Cabbage can be handled like green weed and will keep in a refrigerator. The main difference is that it needs to be 'freshened' every day with immersion in seawater. The cabbage can be either rolled in newspaper or in a hessian bag and kept in the vegie section of the fridge.

Points of Note

The harvesting of cabbage or any bait in the wave break zone of ocean rocks requires extreme caution. Collect the bait only in safe areas and do not work anywhere within the active surf or break zone.

Low tide is always the best time for this type of bait collecting but keep an eye on the sea when anywhere near the water. If the sea is rough, work the rock pools for bait but always exercise extreme care on the ocean rocks.

Luderick are the main target when using green weed.

Green Weed

The magic elixir of estuary luderick fishing, the stringy, filamentous green weed is still sold and sought after as the prime angling bait for these hard fighting fish.

There are at least five or six different types of finely stranded seaweeds that get grouped together as green weed. The different weeds grow in slightly different places but their effect on luderick is roughly the same.

Luderick angling tends to attract a fair number of purist, some of whom insist that one type of weed is superior to all others. While this might occasionally be true, the luderick usually can't spot the difference and eats any of the green weeds, so long as they are well presented.

Where to Find Them

Because there is a variety of green weeds available the places where they can be harvested tends to vary. The most common of the green weeds is found in the intertidal zones of estuaries. It grows on rocks, logs and particularly in tidal drains that feed the bays, or where the drains empty into the bay near a sand or mud bank.

The growth of the weed in the drains may be due to high nutrient flows, increased sunlight or both. Either way tidal drains and natural creeks feeding bays and rivers are always likely gathering spots. The weed tends to cling to the bottom structure and forms a sort of loose matting.

The fine filamentous weed that grows on smooth rocks and timber in the tidal zone is also very useful on luderick. Estuary rock pools often have good growths of this weed. Similarly, many ocean rock pools also have a type of filamentous green weed that is quite acceptable to both ocean and estuary luderick.

Some off-stream areas which are only inundated with saltwater on very large tides can also produce an acceptable weed. Again, this weed tends to be very matted but it will catch the fish.

Take care not to harvest the typical freshwater slime found in some non-tidal pools. This material is useless as bait.

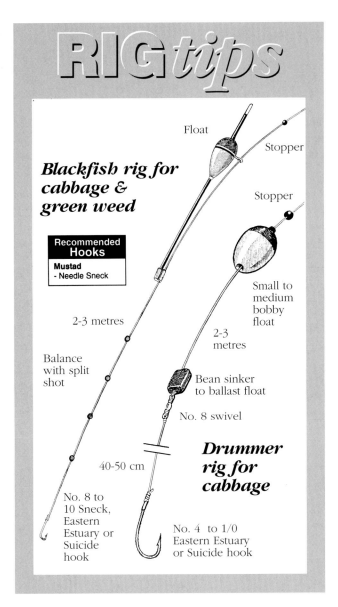

Blackfish rig for cabbage & green weed

Float

Stopper

Stopper

Recommended Hooks

Mustad
- Needle Sneck

2-3 metres

Balance with split shot

Small to medium bobby float

2-3 metres

Bean sinker to ballast float

No. 8 swivel

40-50 cm

Drummer rig for cabbage

No. 8 to 10 Sneck, Eastern Estuary or Suicide hook

No. 4 to 1/0 Eastern Estuary or Suicide hook

Handling Green Weed

Green weed keeps very well in the bottom of the refrigerator just like most vegetables. The best way to keep it is to pack it in small bundles and wrap it in newspaper or roll it in a damp sugarbag as a thin layer perhaps 2 cm thick.

The bag and layer of weed are then rolled and stored in the fridge. The weed can then be 'freshened' every few days by immersing the roll in seawater, allowing it to drain and putting it back in the fridge.

Points of Note

Learning how to keep green weed in good condition is important for anglers who travel to locations away from their usual fishing area. Many places have very good luderick populations but weed is often almost impossible to collect in the same area. The secret is to bring a good supply of weed to the fishing area and this can usually only be done by harvesting and bringing your own. With a couple of 'rolls' of weed the anglers are ready to do battle with as many luderick as care to bite.

The ocean rocks yield good harvest of green weed at times.

Whitebait & frogmouth

Whitebait *(Hyperlophus vittatus)* are a small, readily purchased bait fish that rate highly as a fish taker.

Whitebait are elongated, silvery white in colour and 5 to 10 cm long. They are firm fleshed with a skin covered in small scales. Whitebait are sometimes confused by name with the small glassy which is caught in hoop nets off jetties in coastal estuaries. They are also confused with the New Zealand gourmet food of the same name.

Whitebait are a universally attractive bait to fish that eat other fish. Flathead, tailor, flounder, trevally, salmon, pike, snook, school mulloway and bream are all very keen on these tasty little creatures. Offshore, reef fish, spotted mackerel, bonito, snapper and kingfish will all take them as, will a range of fish off the beach.

Where to Find Them

Whitebait school in large numbers in coastal bays, off beaches and the mouths of estuaries of southern Queensland, New South Wales, South and Western Australia.

Whitebait are netted in the surf and off beaches in deep water harbours and then sent to the bait processors for packaging. They can also be bought fresh from major fish markets.

Strange as it may seem, packaged whitebait are also used quite a bit on freshwater lakes for trout and salmon. The whitebait looks very similar to a number of freshwater bait fish and obviously the trout don't know the difference.

Handling

Like any commercial bait fish, the whitebait in the freezer cabinet is only as good as the handling it was given from the netter who caught it and the processor who packed it. If the fish were iced quickly and packed and frozen soon

---

How to Use Whitebait

Very small whitebait (less than 6 cm), are not much good as they don't stay on the hook very well and are prone to break when baiting up. They are also too attractive to small fish rather than the bigger predators.

Always look for good sized whitebait in the pack. If they are all tiny, leave them in the bait cabinet. The exception is fishing for trout or salmon, then the small ones are fine.

The hooks used to make whitebait rigs are No.1 to 2/0 Limerick patterns. Offset types can be used but they tend to spin in the water.

The real secret of success with whitebait is in its presentation to the fish. It must lie straight and it must appear like a real, live little fish.

The way to do this is to rig it on a pair of linked hooks so that the head of the bait is facing the angler with the second hook in the body of the fish.

The key to this rig is to make sure the top hook is put through the eye of the bait. This holds everything together and allows these small fish to cast very well.

Always measure each bait as it is hooked up, note where the bottom hook needs to be located to ensure the top hook finishes through the eye.

The end result is a bait that lies perfectly straight and looks absolutely natural to the fish.

The bait can also be fished on a single hook but the two linked hooks provide by far the best results. For single hook presentations, just thread a couple of whitebait onto the hook through the eye.

In the estuary, this bait works best when moved either by a drifting boat or by the angler using a slow retrieve. It also works well under a small bobby float when fished for tailor and trevally or drifted with a small running sinker for bream.

There are plenty of flathead anglers who use whitebait for what is known as bait spinning. Fishing a bug or bean sinker right on the hooks and then casting out and slowly retrieving the bait. It is similar to working a lure for flathead and is done in exactly the same places only the retrieve is slower. It is a dynamite technique. Whitebait also works well using the yo-yo technique with either a handline or rod tip.

Of all the baits in the freezer cabinet there are few better than whitebait. Properly rigged and presented they will catch fish.

How to Use Frogmouths

The only drawback with frogmouth pilchards is that sometimes their huge, filter-feeding mouth drops open and causes them to spin and set up a drag against the angler.

Once the mouth pops open they become a problem to use and are usually turned into instant berley. Don't keep using them once the mouth pops open, just toss them into the water.

Despite that one drawback, the frogmouth pilchard is a top bait. Presented on the two hook rig, it is devastating on flathead, tailor and school mulloway plus all the others listed for whitebait.

Some frogmouth pilchards are quite large and many anglers use a three hook gang rather than the two hook rig. It is a matter of personal preference but the third hook may make a difference at times.

The key to using them is exactly the same as whitebait and blue pilchards, have the bait look straight and natural. Adding movement to the bait can also increase captures when seeking predatory fish.

Above: Profile of whitebait and frog mouthed pilchard.
Below: Whitebait and frogmouth presented on double hook and single hook rigs.

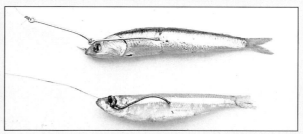

School mulloway are always interested in a well presented whitebait or frogmouth pilchard.

Whitebait & frogmouth casting & spinning rig

No. 2 bug sinker

No. 2/0 linked hooks

35-50 cm trace

Drifting & casting rig

Recommended Hooks

Mustad
- 8260D
- Open Eye 4202D

No. 8 to 12 swivel

No. 2 to 4 bean sinker

No. 2/0 Limerick hooks

Large dusky flathead are regularly caught using either whitebait or frogmouth pilchards for bait.

after capture then they will be a bright, shiny little bait fish with clear eyes and no sign of deterioration or discolouring around the gut cavity.

Poor quality bait fish are not much good anywhere so always reject a packet that looks a bit second hand, whether, it's whitebait, pilchards or whatever. However, whitebait handle packaging better than most baits and are usually in good condition.

Points of Note

As whitebait appeal to all sorts of predatory fish and they keep well, they are worth putting away if you locate a particularly good supply.

Every now and then the bait shop freezer will contain whitebait that are just superb. When found like this go and do the day's fishing and on the way home stop back at the shop and buy a few more packs for the home freezer.

Having a good stock of premium bait is a certain way to help catch more fish.

Frogmouth Pilchards

Another small bait fish of similar dimensions to the whitebait and interchangeable in many ways is the frogmouth pilchard or Australian anchovy *(Engraulis australis)*.

These baits are generally a little bigger than the whitebait and they are almost always purchased from the bait cabinet.

The important differences are that the fish is generally softer, much more oily and spoils much quicker than whitebait.

However, its bright colour and rich oily smell has a definite attraction to some fish. Bream particularly seem keen on frogmouth pilchards.

Handling

The quality of frozen frogmouths tends to vary greatly. As the purchaser you need to be very discerning.

These fish don't keep or handle nearly as well as whitebait. The important thing is to check them carefully before you buy. Make sure they have good colour and that the stomach cavities are not dark or split.

All round though, it is hard to separate whitebait and frogmouth pilchards, both are top baits and they are two of the best baits out of the freezer cabinet.

Worms *beach*

Beachworms belong to the group *Polychaetes* and are easily identified by the presence of bristles projecting from the skin. They are closely related to some of the tube or sand burrowing worms.

For many years fishermen have identified a number of different species and labelled them with a variety of names. Many of these varieties are called blueys, redheads, slimy, kingworm, stumpy, stripy, whitehead, giant and in South Australia bungum worms.

Marine biologists now believe there are at least six different species of beachworms all with their own individual characteristics but for fishermen they all behave the same way and are caught in the same way.

However as it helps to have a specific species to work with the major specie of beachworm both caught and bought is *Australonuphis teres* and can grow to 2.5 metres in length.

Most beachworms have a horny jaw apparatus and this enables them to nip the unwary finger that happens to get in the way. It is something unsuspected by the average person dealing with a 'worm'.

Where to Find Them

The beachworm is found in the active surf zone from Queensland to South Australia. Beachworms on the whole give no visual indication of their whereabouts, however they feed in the sand of the beach slope, using the water movement to bring them food. It is this feeding method which allows for their capture.

To anyone but an angler, the place where worms live would appear devoid of life but just the opposite is true. The same places usually produce pipis, crabs and other shellfish. The sand is deceiving.

Large open surf beaches tend to have the best populations of beachworms though they are present on almost all surf beaches. Even some of Sydney's well known beaches have reasonable numbers of beachworms. The best spots are beaches with a long gentle slope, particularly the shoulders of banks.

How to Catch Them

Beachworms can be caught or bought and this decision is normally based on the available time the angler has. If short of time it is usually better to buy them. Beachworms are sold in most coastal towns but are hard to come by in metropolitan areas because they don't keep well. The packaged live worms only have a shelf life of one to two days, so they rarely travel very far.

To catch beachworms the following is needed. The major requirement is a 'stinky' or worm bait. This is usually a shark head, stingray or a bunch of fish frames either tied together or in an onion bag. The bait is swished through the water on the beach slope as each wave recedes to attract the worms to the surface.

Beachworms are ultra-sensitive to any food item that appears in their area and react instantly by pushing their head out through the sand into the falling water to see if they can find something to eat.

The worm's head comes out of the sand about one centimetre and is easily visible both moving and throwing a distinctive 'V' wake in the dropping surf.

Often, a dozen or more heads will pop up in a small area. At this point, the angler presents a pipi tongue to the worm which it will usually seize firmly with its hard fangs. The tough pipi tongue is usually tied on a short piece of string around the wormers left wrist.

Once the worm is committed to eating the pipi it will arch up trying to get leverage to pull the pipi

Above: Beachworm rigged on Long Shank hook.
Below: Profile of beachworm and worm on hook.

How to Use Them

Beach worms are attractive to a wide range of surf and estuary fish including whiting, bream, dart, flathead, mulloway, flounder, salmon, mullet and tarwhine. As a general rule they are pushed onto the hook by feeding the hook straight down the centre of the body.

The worm is threaded onto the full length of the hook, with the top portion of the worm going over the eye of the hook to help hold it in place. A 3 to 5 cm piece of worm is left hanging below the bend of the hook to provide a fish attracting wiggle. Alternatively, worm pieces are threaded onto the hook until the hook is covered.

The choice of hooks when using beach worms is also critical. Light, fine gauge hooks are best. A fish biting on a beachworm does not expect to find a heavy 'bone' in the middle of it. Long Shanks, Suicides and Eastern Estuary types are all good as are hooks featuring slices and bait holders on the shank.

Beachworms are relatively tough and stay on the hook well during casting, which is important for surf fishing and shore based estuary casting.

Small size hooks are also useful as they make your worms go further if you have to pay for them. If using large beachworms for mulloway baits stay with Suicide patterns for best results.

Beachworms are extremely attractive to surf mulloway particularly on fish from 2 to 10 kg. Use a 4/0 Suicide and pack plenty of worm onto the hook. The 4/0 is big enough to hold a good fish but is small enough to pick up big bream or flathead that take an interest in the bait.

As an all round bait, beachworms are hard to beat, particularly when live and wiggling. They are also great fun to catch.

Beachworms can be kept in dry sand rolled in newspaper.

tongue back into the sand. In some cases the worm can actually be drawn a centimetre or more out of the sand with the pipi tongue. More usually though they just arch up and if the wormer tries to make the worm come too far with the pipi it will just let go and the whole process starts again.

As the worm arches onto the pipi the waiting thumb and forefinger are thrust just under the sand, aiming to grasp the worm just below the white head area. As the worm is grabbed it will release its grip on the sand and shoot its body deeper for a firmer grip. As it shoots its body down the muscle movement is clearly felt and the angler lifts the worm rapidly upwards out of the sand.

While learning, it's not always that easy and sometimes only a portion of the worm is pulled out before it locks itself back into the sand.

Don't pull too hard and break the worm, just hold it in place with constant pressure and have whoever is helping you dig around the body of the worm. Once a few handfuls of sand are removed from around it, the worm will seek another grip and this time it will be pulled all the way out.

With practice anglers soon learn how to pull the worm with one, well timed lift. If in doubt, have someone teach the kids how to catch worms, it is something they can learn fast, it is a challenge and they seem to

enjoy the worming as much as the fishing.

Handling

Beachworms are best stored in a bucket of fresh sea water until collection finishes. They are then placed in dry beach sand and wrapped in newspaper until ready for use. Alternatively, they can be stored in cool seawater in lots of 10 to 20 in plastic bags and kept cool in an ice box with just a few handfuls of ice in it.

If you want to preserve and freeze the worms, drop them into a container of chilled methylated spirits for 15 minutes, drain and place in sealed plastic bags with all air removed. The worms are then placed in the freezer.

Frozen worms are not nearly as effective as live worms but on fish like whiting they are far better than no worms at all. The same goes when buying frozen worms, they work but it is better if you can buy live worms.

Points of Note

In the learning phase, actually getting hold of the beachworm with the fingers can be frustrating. Learning from someone who can show you how it's a bit easier, but mastering that grab through the top layer of sand takes time.

One short cut is to use plastic pliers. The metal ones work but they take the head off the worm too often, the plastic models are the best. The plastic pliers have fat, little teeth loaded into the jaws that allow the worm to be grabbed. The 'feel' for when to lift is not as good but the effect of the pliers on the worms head tends to make them let go of their grip on the sand after a very brief dive for freedom; (can't say I blame them really).

Worms caught with pliers don't last as long as worms caught by hand because of the crushing action of the pliers but they will last a day or so if kept cool.

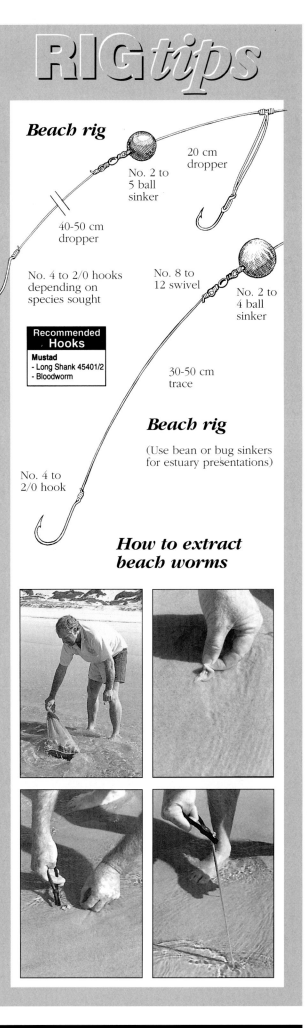

Beach rig

20 cm dropper

No. 2 to 5 ball sinker

40-50 cm dropper

No. 4 to 2/0 hooks depending on species sought

No. 8 to 12 swivel

No. 2 to 4 ball sinker

Recommended Hooks
Mustad
- Long Shank 45401/2
- Bloodworm

30-50 cm trace

Beach rig

(Use bean or bug sinkers for estuary presentations)

No. 4 to 2/0 hook

How to extract beach worms

Worms *blood*

Bloodworms (*Marphysa sanguinea*) are giant mud worms, red to tan in colour and growing to over one metre in length. They are known variously as 'mud worm', bloodworm, or 'Crib Island worm'.

Bloodworms feed on carrion and decomposing material found in mud banks and estuary shorelines where they live in constructed tubes. They also possess a pair of pincer type fangs to assist them in grabbing and holding food.

Bloodworms are softer than beachworms and the name bloodworm comes from the red-black mucus they ooze when broken or placed on a hook.

A small industry also exists supplying bait shops with these worms for those anglers who don't have the time or who don't want the toil of gathering their own bait.

Where to Find Them

Bloodworms are found from southern Queensland to South Australia and they are present in most tidal estuaries deep in the mud or sediment around the border of weed beds, edge of mangrove strands and shell beds. They are most common on intertidal mud flats.

Their location in any area is usually well known at local bait and tackle shops who will give anglers good advice on where to find them. The sight of anglers digging with a pitch fork or spade is always a clear sign of their location and can be used as a starting or reference point.

The worms tend to colonise preferred areas and knowing this is important for harvesting a reasonable quantity for bait, without working too hard.

Unfortunately some of this experience is gained the hard way with a lot of toil for very few worms.

How to Catch Them

The only way to harvest bloodworms is to dig for them with a shovel, spade or pitchfork. It is hard work and one of the reasons many anglers buy their worms despite the expense.

The combination of an hours digging up to the elbows in mudflats is not everyone's idea of fun. However, the rewards are substantial if a good supply of worms is available.

One method that is worthwhile is to turn over any rocks or timber on the mudflat and look for either a fleeing bloodworm or for their telltale silt tunnels laid down in the mud. Once

When digging bloodworms, a worm will often be seen disappearing into the mud. If grabbed quickly by the head it can be steadily drawn out without breakage.

Bloodworm and rigged worm. Note long tailpiece left on bait to attract the fish.

How to Use Them

Putting a worm on a hook is best done by threading the worm onto the hook in a straight line and then leaving a tailpiece below the bend in the hook.

If a big bait is required it is possible to pack the hook by bunching up the worm on the shank. The important thing to remember with this style of baiting is to ensure the point of the hook is left clear so the fish can be hooked easily. Small or broken pieces of worm can also be threaded onto the hook to give the appearance of one worm.

Leaving a tailpiece on the bait gives the worm a very natural appearance and the movement of the tailpiece seems to attract the fish.

One key when using worms is keeping them properly positioned on the shank of the hook. The aim is to cover the hook right to the eye and keep it there during casting and fishing. The best method of keeping the bait in position is to use hooks with slices on the shank. This style of hook often called a 'bait holder' makes fishing with worms easy.

The alternative method of baiting is to thread part of the worm, usually the head, over the eye of the hook. This tends to lock the bait into position but it does not always work as well as bait holder types.

The last point when fishing with bloodworms is to use hook sizes that are economical with the bait. The worms are hard to dig and expensive to buy so look to using smaller size hooks and hooks with shorter shanks. Both points will help to conserve the bait.

signs are found a dig around the area will usually produce a good supply of worms.

It is also important to carefully assess the area you intend to dig. Check that the area has not been turned over recently by another bait gatherer. Look at the ground, changes in surface texture or colour should show what areas have been undisturbed for a long period and what areas have been dug up.

The only accessory needed for gathering worms is a bucket or small cooler for putting the worms in and a hat for sun protection.

Handling

The one drawback of handling bloodworms is their keeping qualities. If not handled with extreme care they putrefy and become useless very quickly.

There are two methods of handling them and both involve thoroughly cleaning the worms in seawater as soon as the digging is finished.

The worms are then placed in a container of seawater and stored in a cool place until needed. Keeping them cool and temperature controlled is vital to producing a good quality bait.

Digging bloodworms is hard, dirty work.

The best place to store the worms is in a fridge running at its least cold setting, about 8°C.

The alternative method is to store the worms in clean, damp but not wet, sand after washing thoroughly. Worms stored this way still need temperature control unless they are to be used quickly after digging.

Points of Note

Digging worms on mudflats is prohibited in some areas, particularly those with environmentally sensitive areas like weed beds. Ribbon weed areas are totally protected in some states and digging them up is a form of eco-vandalism.

Choose your worm digging location carefully and check with the local Fisheries office for further information to find areas which are legally available to you.

Bream and other estuary fish feed keenly on bloodworms.

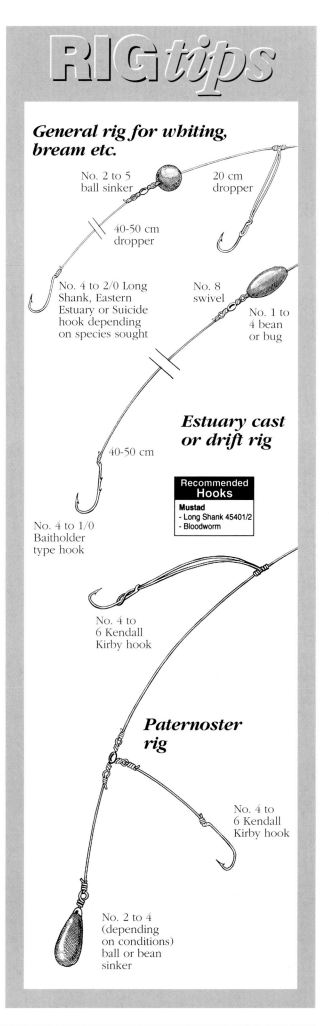

General rig for whiting, bream etc.

No. 2 to 5 ball sinker

20 cm dropper

40-50 cm dropper

No. 4 to 2/0 Long Shank, Eastern Estuary or Suicide hook depending on species sought

No. 8 swivel

No. 1 to 4 bean or bug

40-50 cm

Estuary cast or drift rig

Recommended Hooks
Mustad
- Long Shank 45401/2
- Bloodworm

No. 4 to 1/0 Baitholder type hook

No. 4 to 6 Kendall Kirby hook

Paternoster rig

No. 4 to 6 Kendall Kirby hook

No. 2 to 4 (depending on conditions) ball or bean sinker

Garden worms tend to be so common that many anglers fail to realise their worth as bait. All freshwater fish will eat garden worms.

Because they are common they can also be collected easily and they are equally easy to keep so a source of live bait is always available.

Garden worms as the name suggests are the worms found in lawns and gardens right around the country. They can be very common in areas rich with organic matter and they are also sold by worm farms.

Worm farms also produce a bait worm called red wrigglers which are a small thin worm with distinctive red bands. They are very active when placed on a hook and exude a yellow liquid. For some reason they are attractive to small fish but rarely taken by larger fish.

Where to Find Them

As the name implies garden worms occupy the same environment as humans, they dwell in virtually every lawn and garden.

Places with rich damp soils and lots of organic matter are often well endowed with garden worms. The worms also congregate under ground cover like timber and building materials.

The moist edges of grassy paddocks is also a good spot to look as are banks of top soil.

How to Catch Them

Garden worms are common enough to be simply picked up and put in a worm container either when fossicking in the garden or after periods of rain.

Turning over the garden will usually produce a fair amount but the best way of guaranteeing garden worms is to create a compost heap or mulch a part of the garden which has soft soil and is shady and damp.

Once either the compost or the mulched area is well established the worms will be available whenever needed.

This can be improved further if necessary by creating a worm farm in a plastic bin or old concrete trough. It is also possible to buy a ready made worm farm from many of the enviro shops in capital cities.

Handling

Worms are easily handled and need only ordinary care when transporting to ensure they are kept moist and cool. Keeping them at home in a polystyrene vegetable container or a worm farm in a mixture of soil, vegetable scraps and old lawn clippings works very well.

Profile of red wriggler. or tiger, worm.

How to Use Them

Both garden worms and red wrigglers are used in a similar fashion. Usually the worms are bunched on the hook to make an attractive bait. The best method is to put the hook into the worm about 1.5 cm from the head and then weave it onto the hook two or three times leaving a two centimetre tail piece.

By the time two or three worms are on the hook the bait has lots of wriggling ends to attract the fish.

Large garden worms can be fished singularly by using a small hook like a No.6 or No.8 and these can be used in lightweight fishing for trout or bass.

Both red wrigglers and garden worms are used to 'spice' lures trolled behind Cowbells and Ford Fenders. Often a bunch of worms is trolled on a single hook or a bladed spinner with worms threaded to the trebles is used to 'spice up' the action..

Most often a No.6 or No.4 fly hook is used, loaded with a bunch of worms and trolled dead slow. At times, this is a most effective way of catching trout in the high country lakes.

Presentation under a bubble float works well on all types of freshwater fish. The worms can also be fished on bottom rigs and paternoster type rigs for inland river fish.

Garden worms bunched together.

Bunch of red wrigglers on a hook.

ggler

Trout are the main target species many anglers chase when using garden worms.

The usual trick is to provide a good habitat for them in the yard via a compost heap or mulched area and every month or so round up a bunch of worms and drop them into the worm farm.

When the time comes to go fishing the box is easily turned over and enough

Profile of a garden worm.

worms for the trip are packed into a bucket or lidded container.

If you have a family it is also good fun for youngsters to help with the bait.

Red wrigglers are usually purchased at or near the fishing area but they can also be placed in the worm box or farm.

Like garden worms they will grow and breed in the box and be ready when needed.

Points of Note

Garden worms are a very reliable bait but as a general rule scrub worms are more attractive to the fish. Don't rely entirely on garden worms and try to buy or dig a few scrub worms along the way. By using both types of worms anglers can cover more options.

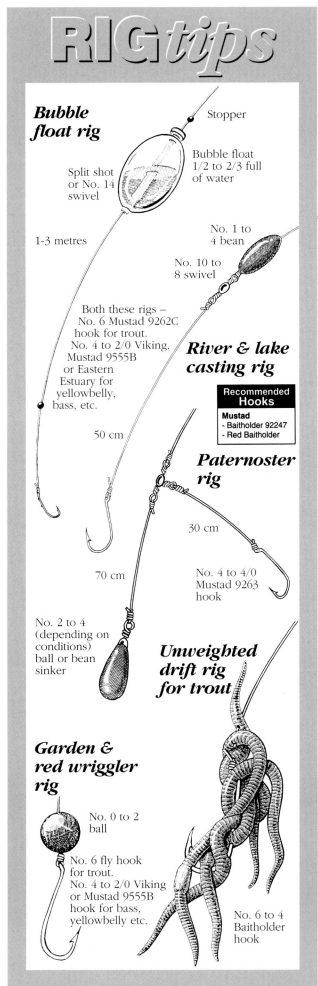

RIGtips

Bubble float rig

Stopper

Bubble float 1/2 to 2/3 full of water

Split shot or No. 14 swivel

No. 1 to 4 bean

No. 10 to 8 swivel

1-3 metres

Both these rigs –
No. 6 Mustad 9262C hook for trout.
No. 4 to 2/0 Viking, Mustad 9555B or Eastern Estuary for yellowbelly, bass, etc.

River & lake casting rig

Recommended Hooks
Mustad
- Baitholder 92247
- Red Baitholder

Paternoster rig

50 cm

30 cm

70 cm

No. 4 to 4/0 Mustad 9263 hook

No. 2 to 4 (depending on conditions) ball or bean sinker

Unweighted drift rig for trout

Garden & red wriggler rig

No. 0 to 2 ball

No. 6 fly hook for trout.
No. 4 to 2/0 Viking or Mustad 9555B hook for bass, yellowbelly etc.

No. 6 to 4 Baitholder hook

Worms *sand & wriggler*

A variety of small worms live in sand and mud banks around the country. These worms have a range of names including tube worms, squirt worms and sand worms.

All these small worms can be caught in basically the same way and for the purposes of this publication are all treated in the same manner.

All sand worms are good bait and can be an important bait supply in many areas. Fish like whiting, bream, flathead, flounder and trevally are all keen takers of these worms.

Where to Find Them

Most of these worms are found on open sandbanks and mudflats. Their location is indicated by small holes and mounds in the sand or by the exposed tubes of secreted mucus and sand that provide a sure sign of a sand worm in residence.

Sand worms tend to colo-nise a favoured bank and large numbers of the worms may be found in one area or in just one part of the sand or mud bank.

Learning the location of such places takes a bit of time and observation but these worms are generally not hard to find if they are available.

Low tide is always the best time to look for sand worms, and the lower the tide the better the chances of finding good supplies of these worms.

How to Catch Them

Most sandworms are caught using a bait pump and often a sieve is needed if working in shallow water. The pump is used in exactly the same way as it is for catching yabbies. The telltale holes in the sand are found, the pump is placed over the hole or group of holes or a sandy tube end if showing and the worms are pumped out with the sand and mud.

This is then sorted and the worms placed in a bucket of fresh seawater.

As a youth one of the authors caught squirt worms by placing an inverted jam tin over the sand beside the worm holes. The jam tin was then stomped on firmly and the air pressure would pop or squirt a worm or two out of the surrounding holes. This same technique is still used today in some places.

The worms can also be dug with a spade or pitch fork but it can be hot, hard work.

Handling

These worms do not handle or keep very well and are prone to break very easily and once broken they don't last very long. It is prefer-able to use them as soon as possible after capture for good results.

The best way to keep the bait is to clean them thor-oughly but don't handle them at all roughly then place them in a container of clean seawater. The worms will also keep in a container of damp seaweed.

As with most live bait, store them in a cool place away from any heat.

Points of Note

There are times when luderick take a big interest in eating small worms, par-ticularly the light coloured squirt worm.

This tends to happen during late autumn and early winter and at times, the worms will outfish an-glers using the more tradi-tional green weed.

The rig remains the same as when fishing with weed only a worm goes on the little hook not a piece of weed. The luderick rig baited with a worm will also take bream at the same time so it can be a handy trick.

Wriggler Worms

Wriggler worms (*Australon-ereis ehlersi*) get their name from the frantic thrashing they produce when freshly dug from the sand and from the constant wriggling when

---

How to Use Sand Worms

The sand worms vary a bit in size but they are mostly small and fairly soft. The key to using them is to use small, light gauge hooks.

The worms are threaded onto the hook covering the shaft and leaving a trailing piece of worm below the bend of the hook. Broken pieces can be put on section by section as needed.

As with all worm baits, hooks with slices on the shank can be a real advantage, keeping the worm firmly posi-tioned during casting and fishing. Baitholder, Suicide, Eastern Estuary and Tru-Turn are all good hooks with this style of fishing.

How to Use Wrigglers

Wriggler worms are both small and thin and are best pre-sented using small, light gauge hooks fished on matching tackle.

The key to success with wriggler worms is to put them on the hook leaving a portion of the hook trailing so its characteristic wiggle can be used to attract the fish.

Bait holder type hooks about No.4 in size are ideal for most wriggler worm presentations. Usually one worm per bait is used unless pieces are being broken up for use on garfish or similar small species.

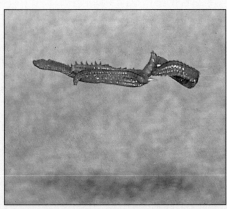

Sandworm rigged correctly on a hook.

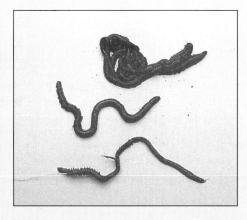

Wriggler worm and rigged as bait. Note use of small, fine hooks.

Southern bream will take sandworm with relish.

placed on a hook.

Wriggler worms are generally tan in colour, though this varies with location, and have two stripes along the back surface. These distinctive little worms make excellent bait.

Growing to an average 12 to 18 cm, wriggler worms are small and fairly thin but many fish are greatly attracted to them. Whiting, bream, flathead, trevally, flounder, garfish and luderick all fall victim to wriggler worms.

They are also relatively easy to dig which adds to their attractiveness.

Where to Find Them

Wriggler worms live near the upper area of the tidal limit mostly in shallow sand and mud areas where they meet with rock shelves. They can also be found under piles of weed, rocks, old logs or any decaying matter.

They particularly favour the sand and mud accumulated in rock shelfs that tend to stay wet during low tide.

They colonise areas in considerable numbers, and once located a lot of wrigglers can be obtained from a small area.

How to Catch Them

As these worms are mostly found in shallow sand and mud often over a rock base, a small spade or garden trowel is the best means of harvesting them.

Usually an area is turned over and the mud sorted for worms which are then dropped into a bucket or small cooler partly filled with seawater.

As these worms tend to gather at the upper tidal limit they can also be harvested at times when other worms on the lower tidal areas are not available. This is worth remembering if you need good bait but the tides do not suit the usual area.

Handling

Wrigglers keep best in damp sand or in seawater. The sand should not be wet at all, just damp, and the worms must be thoroughly cleaned of mud before placing in the sand.

It is also wise to keep only whole worms as these last longer and the broken bits tend to putrefy quickly.

Points of Note

Wriggler worms can break up very easily if handled roughly or if handled when they are thrashing about after their sand dwelling area has been turned over.

Don't try to pick up the worm as it thrashes about. Wait until it is still and then pick it up and drop it into a bucket.

Always remember that whole worms will keep better and be a much better bait when used.

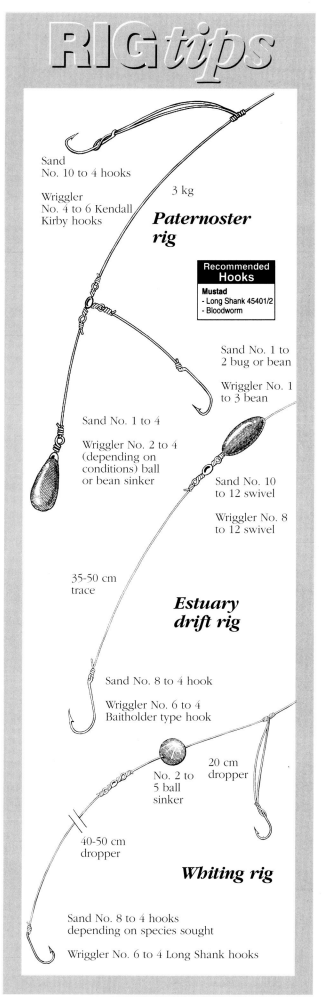

Sand
No. 10 to 4 hooks

Wriggler
No. 4 to 6 Kendall
Kirby hooks

3 kg

Paternoster rig

Recommended Hooks
Mustad
- Long Shank 45401/2
- Bloodworm

Sand No. 1 to 2 bug or bean

Wriggler No. 1 to 3 bean

Sand No. 1 to 4

Wriggler No. 2 to 4 (depending on conditions) ball or bean sinker

Sand No. 10 to 12 swivel

Wriggler No. 8 to 12 swivel

35-50 cm trace

Estuary drift rig

Sand No. 8 to 4 hook

Wriggler No. 6 to 4 Baitholder type hook

No. 2 to 5 ball sinker

20 cm dropper

40-50 cm dropper

Whiting rig

Sand No. 8 to 4 hooks depending on species sought

Wriggler No. 6 to 4 Long Shank hooks

Worms *scrub*

Profile of scrub worms.

Scrub worms are top bait for freshwater catfish.

The humble worm is one of the best fish catchers available to freshwater anglers. Most people are well aware of garden worms but anglers also need to know about the variety of native scrub worms to be found in many areas.

This type of worm varies from place to place, but scrub worms are generally many times larger than the average garden worm and they tend to have much tougher skin. Some of these worms are huge and grow to 60 cm and 1.5 cm thick but on average they are 10 to 25 cm and about half a centimetre thick.

Each area has its own popular species which is fancied by keen anglers. These baits are regularly collected by diggers and sold through the bait shops.

Most scrub worms also contain a sticky mucus which leaks out of the body when placed on a hook. It is thought the fish can smell this mucus from long distances, adding to the attraction of using the worm.

Where to Find Them

Most scrub worms live in moist, loamy soils where there is plenty of organic or decomposing plant material for them to eat.

Many types of scrub worms can be found around the edge of water courses, lagoons or other areas that act as a natural trap for water.

The worms also gather under logs on the ground and can often be found by turning over the timber and then digging under the area where the log had been sitting.

In the inland, look around lagoons and backwaters which are lined with scrub. There is usually a margin of black mud and rotting weeds left as the water recedes. Worms congregate in large numbers under these conditions and can be easily dug from the moist soils.

Around cattle yards are also good spots for worms but always ask permission before entry. The owners

How to Use Them

Scrub worms are attractive to all freshwater fish and are top baits for trout, cod, yellowbelly and catfish.

Using worms is one of the simplest methods of fishing, but careful presentation always helps in attracting and catching more fish.

With scrub worms it is usual to fish one worm per bait as opposed to small garden and red wriggler worms where several worms are needed per bait.

The hook is passed right through the worm from end to end, eventually threading the worm up the line and bringing the hook out half way or more along the body.

Trout anglers often present the worms using one small No.6 hook passed once, straight through the worm from side to side near the head of the worm. This presentation is used when 'floating' the worm along in running water or with a small bubble float suspending the bait.

By hooking the worm once only it wiggles and twists actively making it a prime target for a searching trout.

The more usual rig is a small sinker either sitting right on the hook or using a 35 to 50 cm trace to a swivel and then a sinker.

In inland situations, a paternoster rig with the sinker on the bottom is also useful for holding the bait 30 cm or so off the bottom. Hooks for inland presentations are usually No.2 to 4/0 depending on the fish expected to be encountered.

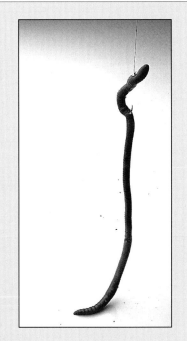

Profile of scrub worm on hook.

Top: Drifting unweighted scrubworms down flooded rivers for trout is a sure fire method. Bottom: Scrub worms are large and robust and make great bait for inland fish.

will also tell you if there are worms present or not anyway.

Wherever scrub worms are dug always ensure that environmental damage is minimised and do not dig out the banks of rivers and streams, work back a little and help minimise the risk of soil erosion.

How to Catch Them

By far the easiest method of obtaining scrub worms is to buy them. The only other option is just plain hard work. Working with a shovel or spade the clods of earth are turned over and dropped so that they break-up a little. Usually one person digs and another sorts the earthy clods for the worms.

Once an area containing worms is established it will usually yield plenty of juicy baits. It can also be used for gathering bait on a regular basis.

The best time to gather worms is generally in the spring or early summer when the ground is still moist and soft. Over summer the ground dries and hardens and the worms can be very hard to find or dig.

Handling

Scrub worms are easy to keep for quite long periods of time provided they are kept in the same soil they were dug from. The worms are stored in large well drained bins or styrene vegetable boxes with drain holes in the bottom.

The worms and their soil are placed into the container along with old composted material. Do not use fresh grass clippings as these decompose they will greatly increase the temperature in the container, killing the worms. This is covered with a slab of damp newspaper and stored in a cool, dry spot. The worms will keep for several months with only a sprinkle of water every couple of weeks and the addition of more composted material.

Points of Note

If fossicking for likely worm areas on private property always make sure the land holder is aware of your intentions. Anglers sometimes turn over large areas of sensitive ground leaving the place looking like the face of the moon and leaving a very bad impression with the land holders.

Take care when on other peoples property and try to leave the ground laid back the way it was before digging the worms. It adds to the workload but it means being able to go back and get more bait the next time.

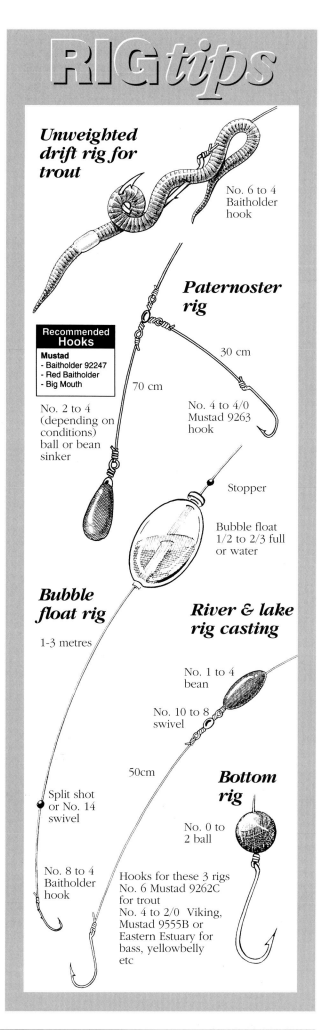

Unweighted drift rig for trout

No. 6 to 4 Baitholder hook

Recommended Hooks
Mustad
- Baitholder 92247
- Red Baitholder
- Big Mouth

Paternoster rig

30 cm

70 cm

No. 4 to 4/0 Mustad 9263 hook

No. 2 to 4 (depending on conditions) ball or bean sinker

Stopper

Bubble float 1/2 to 2/3 full or water

Bubble float rig

1-3 metres

River & lake rig casting

No. 1 to 4 bean

No. 10 to 8 swivel

50cm

Split shot or No. 14 swivel

Bottom rig

No. 0 to 2 ball

No. 8 to 4 Baitholder hook

Hooks for these 3 rigs No. 6 Mustad 9262C for trout No. 4 to 2/0 Viking, Mustad 9555B or Eastern Estuary for bass, yellowbelly etc

Yabbies *freshwater*

Above: Large yabbies can still be used for Murray cod but most are eaten as food by the fisherman.
Right: Yabbies are top bait for yellowbelly.

The freshwater yabby *Cherax destructor* is one of the staple baits of freshwater fishing. These robust little crustaceans are both good bait and good to eat in the larger sizes. They will catch virtually all the main freshwater sportsfish and they can be easily handled and transported.

The boom in farming yabbies for aquaculture does not seem to have produced much of a spin-off for bait seeking anglers but perhaps that will come. There is certainly a demand for the small size yabby in trout waters and demand in other areas could likewise be met by intrepid yabby breeders.

Yabbies are readily caught for bait in most areas including the east coast freshwater rivers and in some cases right in the suburbs, if anglers know where to look.

In inland areas they are very common and most kids of yesteryear have some experience of catching or trying to catch yabbies on a piece of string or line baited with meat. Sadly, not many of today's high tech kids have had the same experience, which is a bit of a pity.

Where to Find Them

As stated, yabbies are present in most freshwater river systems. So long as the water quality is reasonable there will be yabbies around somewhere. In some places where conditions suit them, yabbies can be incredibly thick, to the point of bait stealing any dead or worm baits placed on the bottom.

The best starting place to look for yabbies is in farm dams, particularly those that feed the headwaters of small creeks. On coastal creeks it is the small pools of tributary creeks which hold the most yabbies.

In the Murray/Darling basin many of the rivers are

How to Use Them

There are really only two ways of putting a yabby on a hook. Live yabbies are set with the hook through the second or third segment of the tail. The hook goes from the underside and out the top.

The hooking process keeps the bait alive for a very long time and presents the bait very naturally with the hook point clear and exposed to strike at the fish.

Small yabbies used as trout baits are usually presented under bubble floats. The smaller the yabby the better on trout, with little 2 and 3 centimetre models being devastating. Yabbies of all sizes will be taken by the trout, it just depends on the size of the trout, though baits up to 8 cm are the best. The same rig and technique can also be used on bass.

On inland fish live bait presentations are still popular although the float is usually abandoned for a small ball sinker running right to the hook or a paternoster rig which keeps the yabby suspended off the bottom. Both rigs can be used to 'bob' around snags and other likely spots. Bobbing is moving the bait up and down to attract a strike from any fish in the area.

In inland waters yabbies are also fished peeled with the head and tail shelled to allow the juices to attract the fish. Some anglers just crush or remove the carapace

Yabby on hook.

(shell) around the head to achieve the same effect. The bait is placed on the hook whole, running the hook from the tail and bringing the point out where the abdomen joins the legs. The top part of the shell is then removed.

Hook sizes depend on the size of the bait and the size of the fish being sought. For trout No.6 or No.4 is about right though No.1 size hooks may be used on larger baits. For native fish, hooks from No.2 to 4/0 are suitable.

boarded by irrigation channels or lagoons and these are the best places to find yabbies rather than in the rivers themselves. However, there are always some yabbies in the rivers.

In the alpine lakes there are also plenty of yabbies, particularly around stands of drowned timber and weed beds.

Yabbies are not very common during winter as they hibernate but emerge as soon as the warm weather starts.

How to Catch Them

Using the meat on a string trick still works but it can be a bit slow. The best results come from using a scoop net pulled through the shallows of a lagoon, irrigation drain or farm dam.

Quiet, environmentally healthy farm dams are usually the best bet for a good supply of yabbies.

Fold out shrimp traps also work though the purpose designed opera house yabby trap is about the best on large size yabbies.

Small yabbies are often easily caught in hoop nets made with fine mesh.

Whichever trapping method is used, several traps are needed, relying on just one will not usually yield enough yabbies for a good bait supply.

The traps are baited with raw meat or fish heads although plenty of exotic recipes exists in the bush. Raw meat seems as good as anything and is never a problem to obtain.

Profile of yabby.

Handling

Yabbies can be kept alive for months as long as they are in a tightly lidded container and stored in a cool place.

They are best kept in a styrene vegetable box with just enough water to leave their backs exposed is about right. Check every couple of days and remove any dead yabbies as they will send the water putrid killing all the occupants.

Don't feed them meat either, just a few teaspoons of grated carrot every week is fine. Change the water every two weeks.

Alternatively, the crayfish can be kept in a freshwater aquarium but give them plenty of places to hide or cannibalism can break out rapidly. Again grated carrot is the best food.

Being fairly tough and robust the yabbies handle capture and transport very well. Be careful with them though as rough handling can still damage them and as with all live bait, high temperatures will kill them very quickly.

Points of Note

Any live yabby fished on the bottom will instinctively try to find cover by crawling under or onto any log or hole available.

This can be stopped by either suspending the bait off the bottom or by keeping the bait moving slowly. Alternatively the nippers can be removed from the yabby which will stop it crawling very far.

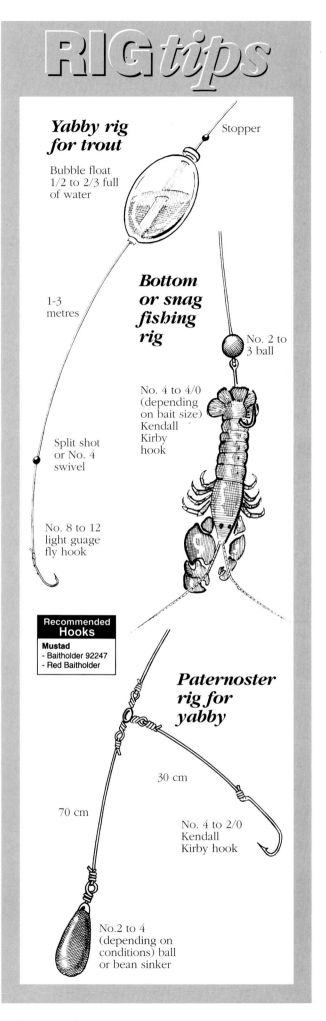

Yabbies *saltwater*

Pumping yabbies is always great fun for kids.

Areas rich in yabbies are usually rich in fish as the tide rises.

Yabby bank with their holes clearly visible.

The saltwater yabby has collected a range of names around the country leading to occasional confusion for readers of angling publications.

Apart from the common term 'yabby' which gets it confused with the much larger freshwater crustacean, this shrimp is also know as a 'bass yabby' in Victoria, a 'pink nipper' in New South Wales and a ghost shrimp by students of marine biology.

With all these titles it's no wonder anglers get confused. The animal goes by the scientific name of *Callianassa australiensis*, though its common title of nipper is also suitable as it can inflict a painful pinch with its over-sized right claw.

The saltwater yabby is one of the best baits available, just about everything that swims in an estuary or along the rocks will eat it. Fish like bream, flathead, whiting, flounder, trevally and school mulloway find them irresistible.

On the ocean rocks, in addition to taking bream and trevally they are a top bait for drummer.

This bait works because it is extremely attractive to a wide range of fish and it is usually fished alive which makes it doubly attractive. There is also something about its colour which seems to draw the fish.

The only fault that yabbies have is their attraction to small pickers. Bait losses can be high if little whiting or bream are thick.

Where to Find Them

Yabbies tend to colonise preferred sandbanks and sandflats. They are located by looking for the telltale holes they make in the sand. These holes provide a source of protection from their many natural enemies. Underground, they use the 'swimmers' on their legs to move water through their burrows to both breathe and feed.

Many thousands of yabbies will be located in a particular area and in some cases vast expanses of intertidal flats may be well populated by these shrimp.

Some of these spots have become famous as bait collecting areas. The location of good yabby banks in any area is generally known. Most tackle shop proprietors and local anglers should be able to suggest the best spots. Even so, it pays to keep a lookout for their holes in the sand when out fishing as many top yabby grounds are overlooked or can only be reached by boat.

How to Catch Them

To catch yabbies the angler needs nothing more than one of the stainless steel suction pumps available from almost every tackle shop in the country. A bucket to hold the little beasties and a large sieve, if prospecting on submerged sandflats.

The yabby pump is placed over a selected hole or holes in the sand and the handle lifted rapidly. At the same time, some downward pressure is exerted on the tube. A mud and sand core is then extracted and the contents sprayed in front of

How to Use Them

Putting the yabby on a hook takes a little care and hook sizes need to match the physical dimensions of the yabby.

The best hooks tend to be small and of light gauge. Long Shanks around No.4 size are ideal for whiting while Suicide type patterns are also good. Hooks with sliced shanks have added capacity to hold the bait in place and do work well on yabbies. Some of the chemically sharpened hooks available are also worth trying, again because they have strong, light gauge hooks in their range.

The baits are rigged by feeding the yabby onto the hook from the tail end with the hook following the underside and emerging when three or sections of the body are on the hook. Rigged this way the bait looks natural and will present enticingly to any fish that takes an interest.

If using small hooks or large yabbies (they can grow to 10 cm), then just run the hook through as many segments as will fit and then gently pull the eye of the hook into the tail segment, this will lock the bait onto the hook.

It is also possible to thread the yabby on, then turn the hook right around and push the barb back through the yabby and out through the top of its back. This holds the yabby really well but only works with large size yabbies.

Always cast yabbies carefully. They are not a tough bait and a wild swing or miscast can see the rig go one way and the yabby the other. Careful presentation of the bait is vital.

Yabbies set on hooks must sit straight and look natural..

the pumper or waiting assistant. The yabby or yabbies are then plucked from the expelled sand and mud and placed in a bucket half filled with sea water.

When pumping yabbies it is important to work with the tide. Most yabby banks will be available from about half tide down to half tide up. Yabbies can be harvested from deeper water by using a sieve supported by an inner tube to separate the baits from the sand.

When pumping yabbies pick them up carefully. They are quite fragile and can be easily damaged if handled roughly. Remember it is important to keep the bait alive for best results.

When young children help with the yabby collection, which they usually love, make sure the kids know they have to handle the bait with care and that the large nipper out front can inflict a nasty bite. The bite usually does nothing more than bruise, but it will hurt a youngster, ruining their fun for the day.

Profile of yabbies.

Handling

It is necessary to follow a few simple rules when keeping yabbies for bait. Yabbies like all living things have to breathe. If too many yabbies are in a bucket they may exhaust the oxygen available and die quite quickly.

This can be solved by either frequent water changes or by adding an aerator. If the bait is to be used quickly after capture then a change of water every 20 to 30 minutes is fine.

Keeping the bait overnight or for later use needs a little more thought. First, all dead or badly injured yabbies must be removed from the bucket. Dead yabbies will send the water putrid killing all the other yabbies quite quickly.

The second issue is water temperature. In the sea, the temperature is relatively stable and sudden rises or falls will kill yabbies and other marine creatures. For this reason, most anglers use a medium sized cooler for storage. The insulated cooler or ice box also has greater surface area than a bucket meaning more oxygen for the yabbies.

The cooler should always be stored out of the sun in a cool, shady spot.

With a change of water twice a day the yabbies will keep for at least 2 days and sometimes longer.

Points of Note

When pumping yabbies other baits such as worms, prawns and small crabs are also brought to the surface and all make good baits.

Never overlook the place where the yabbies are pumped as a likely fishing spot. Many fish will feed over the area at high tide and more particularly at night. During daylight, look at any deep drop-offs close by the yabby banks as a likely spot for holding fish during low tide.

Many anglers also fish while the yabby pumping is in progress, either with someone allocated to do the fishing (tough job), or by setting a rod in a sand spike while they walk around pumping.

As a bait for almost all estuary species the yabby takes a lot of beating. Being live and freshly caught adds to the attraction. It is a proven fish catcher and is itself good fun and good exercise to catch.

No. 0 to 2 ball sinker

No. 4 to 2 Suicide or Eastern Estury hook

Bream rig also used for jetty & rock fishing

No. 1 to 3 bean or bug sinker

No. 8 to 12 swivel

35-50 cm

Estuary drift & casting rigs

Recommended **Hooks**
Mustad
- Baitholder 92247
- Red Baitholder

No. 6 to 2 Baitholder or Long shank

Yellowtail

Profile of yellowtail.

Yellowtail *(Trachurus novaezelandiaeare)* is one of the most common and most versatile fish baits available. They can be used as live bait, whole dead baits, filleted and cut into strips or butterflied by removing the spine.

The fish is abundant in both estuaries and offshore and is one of the more common captures from harbour jetties in temperate waters.

Yellowtail are part of the scad family. They are a school fish, often congregating in large numbers. They are also an important food item for many inshore fish like mulloway, snapper, tailor, bonito, yellowtail kingfish (no relation), flathead, hairtail and many others.

Where to Find Them

Yellowtail can be found in most estuaries, along the rocky coast and around offshore reefs out to at least 80 metres.

In the estuaries they regularly school around wharves, pylons, sea walls and other man-made structures. They also congregate over weed beds, along drop-offs and at the ends of deep bays.

Offshore, the fish gather over kelp beds, along headlands and particularly in deep, sheltered coves.

Further offshore, yellowtail school in big numbers around many reefs and they can often be located using a sounder.

How to Catch Them

Yellowtail bite readily and are generally easy to catch although they do become educated in hard fished waters.

The fish are readily attracted by berley such as pulped wet bread, soaked dog biscuits or soaked chicken pellets and pulped fish from a berley bucket. The berley attracts the fish and holds them in the area and it also seems to stimulate them to bite more readily.

The fish are usually caught using a light 2 or 3 kg handline with a No.6 to No.10 hook with just a tiny split shot crimped onto the line 20 cm from the hook. The choice of hook size is determined by the size of the bait being sought. The smaller the yellowtail the smaller the hook size needed to catch them.

Yellowtail will keenly attack a bait jig and many anglers rely on these devices for their bait supply. The jigs are often 'spiced' with small strips of yellowtail or pinches of prawn to give them extra appeal.

In shallow water the fish can be easily attracted to the berley and caught with baited lines or bait jigs. In deeper water and around offshore reefs, bait jigs are the most effective way of catching yellowtail.

Handling

Yellowtail are a tough, durable bait and they stay alive very well in a bait tank or aerated bucket.

The fish are generally more effective when used alive and setting up a live

How to Use Them

Putting a live yellowtail on a hook, as with any live bait, takes care and attention to detail. Always choose a hook that suits the size of the bait being used. A big hook will quickly kill a small bait fish. The fish will also last longer and be more attractive to predators when fished on a small yet strong hook.

As with all live bait it is vitally important to keep the hook away from the lateral line which is clearly marked on each side of the yellowtail. If a hook is placed through this area the bait will die quickly.

In most situations, the yellowtail works best when hooked through the shoulder close to where the dorsal spines are located or through the nose, just in front of the eyes. Baits hooked in the tail area will catch fish but tend to die quickly as they are held back to the current and down. In heavy current the nose rig always works best.

Above left: Hook-up positions for yellowtail.
Left: Yellowtail whole and prepared as butterfly bait.

Yellowtail caught on a bait line.

bait storage system makes handling them easy.

Don't put too many in the tank unless there is a constant exchange of sea water to keep them going. Usually a dozen or so in an aerated bucket is about right.

If the baits are to be used dead as fillets, strips or whole baits, drop them into a mixture of ice and sea water so they are in prime conditions for later use or for freezing.

Points of Note

One little trick that improves

results when using dead yellowtail is to turn the baits into butterflies.

This involves carefully filleting the bait from the tail towards the head but stopping just short of the stomach cavity. The fish is sliced on both sides and the spine and tail is gently removed.

The bait is hooked through the nose and is fished with a yo-yo type technique which makes the sides of the fish flutter as if wounded as it rises and falls.

Butterfly baits are deadly on flathead, mulloway, yellowtail kingfish and teraglin.

Yellowtail prepared for strip bait.

Rig for catching yellowtail

Handline or light reel

3 kg line

No. 6 to 10 Long Shank hook

No. 0 to 1 split shot 25cm from hook

Stopper

Strips of fish bait or pieces of prawn

Light float or quill

Recommended Hooks
Mustad
- Long Shank 45401/2
- Bloodworm

Stopper

Medium bobby float

Float rig for mullet garfish & yellowtail

Balance with split shot

2-3 metres

1 to 2 metres

Ball sinker for ballast

No. 8 swivel

50 cm

No. 8 to 12 Long shank hook

No. 3/0 to 8/0 Suicide or Live Bait hook

Surface fish, offshore, off rock, or jetty rig

Recommended Hooks
Mustad
- Big Gun
- Hoodlum

25 kg trace

No. 2 to 4 bean sinker

No. 6 swivel

10 to 25 kg line

40 to 50 cm

Mulloway rig

No. 4/0 to 8/0 hook

Bait *jig rigs*

Of all the new fishing products that constantly flood onto the Australian market, only a relative handful ever find a real niche here. One such item has been the Japanese bait catching jig rig - the most effective bait catching device yet invented, and a tackle item that has changed the way many Aussie anglers go about procuring their live baits.

There is nothing very complicated about these jigs, in fact they are simpler to use than many conventional bait fishing methods when it comes to catching live baits, and it is this simplicity and their incredible effectiveness at catching so many different types of bait fish that has earned them widespread acceptance among anglers.

What Exactly Are They?

So what exactly are they? Basically, bait catching jig rigs are sets of small white, pearl or pink flies attached to small droppers at evenly spaced intervals along a length of relatively heavy monofilament line.

Each complete, packaged rig usually carries six flies. So effective are these devices, that it is not unusual for every one of those flies to get taken by a bait fish. To avoid tangles when bringing a "full house" of

bait fish on board, many anglers cut the rigs in half and fish a shorter rig with only three or four flies at one time.

How to Rig Them

Bait catching jig rigs usually measure around 1.5 metres in length. The line is tied to one end, normally by way of a swivel, and a sinker is attached to the other end to provide casting weight or for carrying the rig down to where the bait fish are schooling.

Each fly or jig consists of a small piece of coloured material which is exceptionally tough and will outlive the small hook to which it is tied. Most have a bright orange or red head with a small luminescent bead running down to it. The material used in the flies of the best bait rigs is dried eel or fish skin.

The flies are also tied to stand off the main line. This should be checked before tying the jig on. Hold the jig one way up then the other. The way that stands off the trace is the right way.

Bait jig rigs can be purchased in a range of hook sizes with the correct selection being based on what bait are being sought.

Generally, the smallest size is best for catching yellowtail, garfish, small slimy mackerel, herring, pilchards

and the like, while larger sizes are recommended for catching larger slimies, cowanyoung and even small tuna such as bonito and frigate mackerel.

Bait Fish and Jigs

Just about any species of small bait fish - along with some real surprises - will respond to jig rigs so long as they are fished with the right technique. Principal candidates for bait rigs are any of the bait fish usually employed as live baits for catching larger predators. These include yellowtail, cowanyoung, slimy mackerel, garfish, herring, nannygai, pike, hardyheads, mullet and pilchards. Larger bait jig munchers - which often prove just too powerful for the small jig rigs and only serve to break hooks - include very large slimy mackerel, bonito, frigate mackerel, tailor, salmon, small kingfish, trevally, barracouta and snapper. Unwanted species such as sweep, mados and various small rock dwellers also regularly pounce on a bait jig, particularly if they are worked deep down over areas of heavy reef.

Bait jig rigs can be purchased in a number of jig and hook sizes. Generally, the smallest size 10 or 8 models are the best allround ones, although where

Small bonito are often caught on bait jigs.

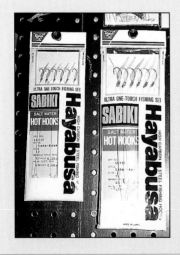

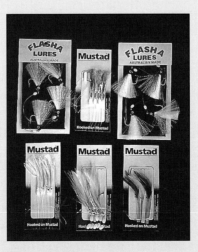

How They're Sold

Bait jig rigs can be purchased at most tackle stores, and cost between $1 and $4 each, depending on their size and style. For most anglers who depend on live baits for their fishing and who regularly purchase bait jig rigs, these items are usually regarded as expendable. They tangle badly once unwrapped, and are difficult to store.

Once the hooks - which are weak on most jig rigs - have been broken or rusted, they should be discarded and another couple of rigs purchased to replace them.

Far left: Hayabusa bait jigs.
Left: Flasha and Mustad bait jigs.

Bait jigs come in a wide variety of sizes.

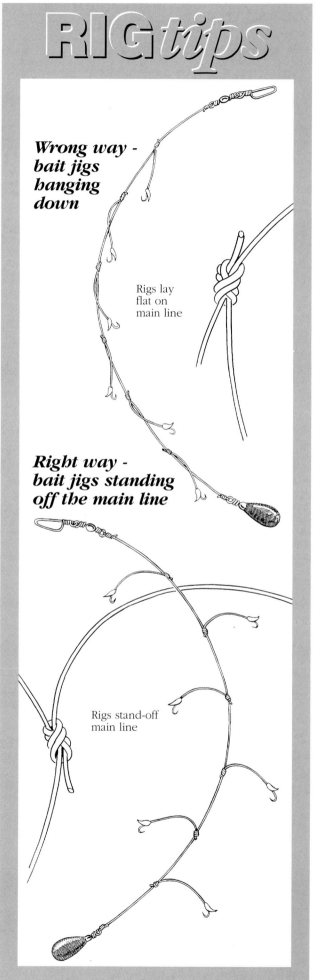

Wrong way - bait jigs hanging down

Rigs lay flat on main line

Right way - bait jigs standing off the main line

Rigs stand-off main line

larger bait fish predominate, larger jigs with stronger hooks around size 6 to 2 are a wise investment. The larger jig rigs can also be slow trolled around known bait grounds with success.

Most anglers prefer the snapper or teardrop shape sinker for distance casting and attaining a quicker sink rate of the jig.

How to Fish the Jig Rigs

The success of bait catching jig rigs is reliant as much on the actual jig design itself as it is on the method that is used to fish them. In reality, these small jigs or flies are actually mini lures and they need to be given action by the angler to be productive.

As with bait fishing for yellowtail, slimies and the like, berley is always a great asset, and often vital to the success of bait rigs, particularly where the bait is frequently haunted by anglers and larger predatory fish alike.

Bait rigs should be fished with a slow jigging action. Often, the movement of an anchored boat is sufficient for achieving this action and a bait rig can be set from a rod holder; the rod tip bobbing up and down and providing sufficient movement

to the jigs to induce a strike.

Once one bait fish is hooked on a jig rig, often before you can wind it in, all the other hooks will get taken and a 'full house' of lively bait fish is the pay-off.

But the most widely practised method is to jig the bait rig at the same level as where the bait fish are stationed in the water column. From the rocks, and especially when the sun is up and there is bright light streaming on the water, bait fish will hang deep, so the rig may need to be worked right near the bottom.

As a final pointer, if the bait fish are proving particularly finicky and shy, try individually spicing each jig with a small piece of fish flesh, ideally a tougher section of bait with the skin attached.

Bait catching jig rigs really are quite an incredible tackle innovation. Knowledgeable land-based and boat-based anglers who regularly use live baits for nailing big predators, are indirectly catching more fish through the time saving benefits gained by catching their bait with these devices.

Wherever bait fish need to be procured, look no further than bait jig rigs......you'll be pleasantly surprised.

Presentation *is the key*

Good bait, even live bait can be enhanced in its fish catching ability by good presentation to the fish.

While most anglers have particular ideas of how a bait should go on a hook, there are methods available that genuinely produce more fish than others.

The secret is to present a bait which the fish like to eat in a manner which the fish finds attractive and wants to eat.

Educated Fish

In some heavily fished waters the fish are highly educated about hooks, heavy sinkers and second rate bait. Anything they regard as suspicious is given a wide berth and only anglers who take care to get everything right will have success.

The 'tourist resort' bream is famous as a canny adversary. These fish have seen too many smelly prawns curled up double on an oversize hook with the rig anchored to the bottom by a lump of lead.

The same fish presented with a live prawn hooked lightly in the tail with a No.2, light gauge hook and on a rig that lets the bait move around a little, will pounce on the live bait and be hooked.

The key to making good bait produce the best possible result is to use good presentation. Good presentation makes the bait look natural and easy to eat and it is complemented by good rigs which enhance the look of the bait and allow the fish to eat the bait easily.

Hooks

Hooks are one of the vital tools of trade for anglers. In the game of bait presentation they are the most important weapon. Selection of appropriate hook patterns for both the bait being used and the fish being sought are extremely important parts of the fish catching equation.

As an example, the use of worms or yabbies on whiting has some considerations that need to be made to select the right hook. These same considerations can be applied to almost any fish or bait in hook selection.

Firstly, whiting have a very small mouth, do not grow very big and can be very shy biters, also, they have no teeth or sharp spines.

Favourite baits are worms, yabbies and shellfish all of which are basically small baits.

Given all of the above the best hook for whiting will be small, say a No.4. The shape of the hook will be better if it has a long shank to support both the yabby and worm but a shorter shanked hook could be used when shellfish are the bait. Something like a Viking or Baitholder pattern would work well.

The long shank type pattern is also easier to get out of this small mouthed, long snouted fish.

Care and attention to detail produces baits that fish want to eat.

The final play in this game is to put the bait on the hook so that it appears as attractive as possible to the fish. This means keeping the yabby straight so the legs and nippers can move about and the body is not contorted. Having the yabby bent double around the hook is not how whiting or any other fish is used to seeing this bait.

With worms its much the same, keep the worm straight on the shank and leave a piece trailing and wriggling seductively.

Baiting the Hook

One of the great misconceptions that many anglers have about bait is that the whole bait has to be on the hook. Nothing could be further from the truth and nothing leads to more baiting foul-ups than this idea.

Curling a prawn or yabby right around a hook or trying to put on a strip of fish flesh by threading the hook several times through the strip are two of the great mistakes of bait fishing.

Prawns, yabbies, nippers and others only need to be held straight and natural on the hook. How much of the bait is actually on the hook has almost nothing to do with hooking the fish. Making the bait look right is far more important than trying to hide the hook.

The methods shown in this book provide answers that show the best presentation combined with the best hook-up ratios. The thing to remember is that presentation comes first. No hook-ups can occur unless the fish is attracted to the bait first.

The point on using fish strips is also vital. The best strip baits are usually presented with the hook passed once through the bait from the flesh out through the skin.

Passing the hook through the strip several times may make it hard for the fish to get the bait off the hook but it can also cause the bait to end up all bunched up around the bend of the hook. This leaves the point

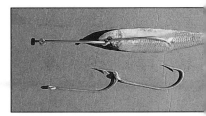

Whitebait on a double hook rig looks natural and tempting to the fish.

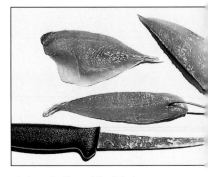

A sharp knife and fresh bait can produce very useable fish strips.

of the hook surrounded by bait making it impossible to hook the fish.

With a hook passed once only through a fairly thin strip of bait, the fish can swallow it easily and be well hooked by the fully exposed point of the hook. Strip baits that look just like the little bait fish they are imitating get treated and eaten like a little bait fish.

Ganged Hooks

Many bait presentations can be enhanced by using several hooks ganged together. The classic tailor and salmon rig with a garfish or pilchard relies on ganged hooks for success but there are many other baits that can benefit from using ganged hooks.

Whitebait, frogmouthed pilchards and a whole range of small fish can be attractively presented using ganged hooks. Strip baits, whole squid, octopus tentacles and other baits can be rigged on ganged hooks.

Not only do these rigs enhance the presentation of the bait they also add to its ability to hook and hold the fish.

Live Baits

Using live bait takes in a range of variables that need to be combined to make what are essentially the very best of baits as appealing as possible to the fish.

The most important part is to match the hook size to the bait size and also the gauge and thickness of the hook to the size of the bait. Putting a big hook into a small live bait will both look unnatural and probably kill the bait quickly.

A small yellowtail or herring can easily carry a 3/0 or 4/0 size hook, but a 10/0 would kill it. However, the 10/0 could easily be handled by a big yellowtail or slimy mackerel. It is all a matter of proportion and the hook should always be related to the live bait rather than to the fish that is likely to eat the live bait.

Modern technology ensures that even quite small hooks like a 3/0 or 4/0 Live Bait pattern can handle fish to 30 kg. It is a matter of balancing the hook to the tackle as well as to the bait.

The other important point with live bait is that they are mostly eaten head first and this is where the hook should be placed.

Apart from being in the strike zone, baits hooked in or near the head will drift better and hold better in a current than those hooked further down or along the body.

In fact, baits hooked near the tail will drown rapidly when towed backwards by drifting or held backwards in the current. Baits should only be hooked near the tail if required to swim away from a particular spot and when fished in relatively still water.

Most live baits are hooked from side to side through the nose or from under the bottom jaw and out through the top of the snout. The other favoured spot is through the top of the back just behind the head about where the small spines start on the dorsal fin.

This particular type of hooking arrangement is ideal for working live baits under floats as it lets them move around in a natural manner.

Offshore anglers use either of the hooking methods depending on location and the amount of current in the spot being fished. Both methods work, but nose rigs are used in spots with strong currents and back rigs are used in spots with no or low current.

Catching large mulloway requires skill in both bait rigging and in presentation.

Summary -
Mustad Premium & Standard Hooks

Hook Type/Pattern	Standard	Premium (Chemically Sharpened)
Kirby	4190/4200	-
Limerick	8260D	-
Tarpon	7766D	Red Tarpon
Open Eye Ganged hooks (1/0 +)	4202D	
Open Eye Ganged hooks (4 to 1)		Needle Tarpon Open Eye
Suicide light	9263	
Suicide 2x strong	92554	Big Red
Baitholder	9262C 9555/9555B	
Baitholder long shank	92247	Red Baitholder
Live bait heavy	9175D	Hoodlum
Live bait general		Big Gun
Long shank	4540 1/2	Bloodworm
Long shank stainless	92608	
Wide Gap	37140	Big Mouth
Fly hooks	94840	80000
Fly hooks - long shank	9672	
Sneck	3331	Needle Sneck

Hook Study Important

Whether using a live bait or a piece of shellfish the choice of hook will impact on the way the bait is presented and how it responds when a fish is hooked.

The choice of hooks now available is vast. New hook types and patterns are appearing all the time. The traditional patterns have been vastly improved by technological advances in manufacturing technique. In competition to the traditional hooks have come the chemically sharpened hooks which have provided new shapes and sharper hooks to help anglers.

Many hooks are actually quite blunt straight from the box and need to be sharpened with a stone or file before use but chemically sharpened hooks are razor sharp straight from the pack. Overall, hooks are of excellent quality and it is up to the angler to choose those patterns and sizes that suit the fishing being done and the bait being used.

Experimenting with different hook types can help improve captures and bait presentations and each angler needs to spend a little time trying to get their own fishing system right.

It is publications such as this that can help to stimulate ideas and show how others apply hooks and rigs to catch more fish more often. There are few things that are more fun than learning something new and then going out and trying it on the fish. Being rewarded with success only reinforces the learning process.

Bait *collecting gear*

Offshore anglers rely heavily on live baits which they draw to the back of a boat using finely mashed berley.

H aving good bait or live bait is a key ingredient to making catches of quality fish. Today's busy world has reduced the available fishing time and bait gathering time for many anglers.

This has placed increased reliance on packaged and frozen baits, most of which are of high quality but in some cases nothing beats having live or really fresh bait.

The modern bait shop has come a long way too. Many carry live worms, yabbies, shrimp, prawns and the freshest of fresh garfish, pilchards, whitebait and small tuna. Knowing that the shop has good live or fresh bait can be a big help but sometimes there is no other way to get the bait other than to catch or collect it yourself.

Bait collecting is one of the skills of fishing. Good bait gatherers are usually competent anglers and learning about bait also teaches many lessons about the fish being targeted.

A wide range of equipment is available to collect various baits. Each piece of gear has some application to a facet of bait catching, just choose what is necessary for the bait required.

There are regulations covering bait gathering equipment in each state and anglers need to check with their local Fisheries office just what bait gathering equipment they can and cannot use.

Bait nets and cast nets are only legal in Queensland, the Northern Territory and Western Australia but some other gear is also limited and needs to be checked.

Bait Traps

There are two distinct types of bait traps available. One is a clear plastic tube with small funnel holes at each end and the other type is made of a fine mesh netting with tapered funnels at each end and a bait bag on top.

Both types work although they tend to work better on slightly different species.

The clear plastic types are excellent for catching small mullet and other fish in shallow bays and near weed beds or wherever small mullet are seen.

The clear trap is baited with bread and left on the bottom (a sinker or small rock may need to be added for this). The area is 'seeded' with finely mulched wet bread to attract the mullet and get them feeding. Usually they will enter the trap within 15 minutes or so and when feeding avidly will actually pack the trap with little fish.

The mesh bait nets will work on mullet and other small fish but they seem to

Clear plastic bait traps are very useful for catching mullet and other small fish for bait.

A portable live bait tank with attached aerator makes great sense for shore based fishermen.

Live bait tanks are a key component in most fishing boats.

This live bait or live shrimp or yabby container can be left in the water or in its matching bucket.

Above: Bait nets make catching small fish easy.
Below: Bait net loaded with hardyheads ready for use.

Bait Nets

A bait net is usually made of 3 cm mesh and is between 8 and 30 metres long with a 2 metre drop. It has a leadline at the bottom, a cork or float line at the top and a pole at each end. It is operated by two people, each one holding a pole affixed to the end of the net.

Beginning at one end of a beach, the two operators walk along in the shallow water dragging the net. As they approach the other end of the beach, they gradually come closer and walk up the beach, to find, hopefully, that the net is full of bait fish. The bait is usually kept alive, if possible, in a bait tank or bucket.

Cast Nets

A cast net is a cone of netting, meshed in such a way that it will lie flat when spread. The cone of the cast net is fitted with a leadline around its perimeter. These lead weights should be spaced so that they cannot pass through the mesh of the net and cause tangles.

A nylon or cotton cord is spliced to the apex of the cone and used for retrieving the net. The length of the cord can vary. For normal use it should be around 4 metres long. A shorter cord can be used from a boat, whereas a longer cord would be needed when casting from heights such as a wharf or jetty. The free end of the cord has a loop, large enough to fit over the wrist.

For all-round use, the recommended net size or drop is 2.5 metres with a mesh size of 3 cm. Smaller nets with a drop of 1.5 metres are available for junior anglers.

Cast nets are not legal in every state but they make catching small fish and prawns very simple.

Once the art of handling and casting a cast net is mastered, it is almost always possible to catch a good supply of fresh bait fish such as mullet, herring, pilchards, garfish and prawns.

Prawn Drag Nets

Prawn drag nets are a very useful legal means of catching bait. Catching prawns of both table and bait quality is what the nets are designed for and they do this very well but they also catch squid, small fish and other useful bits and pieces.

The drag nets are usually 6 metres long with a 2 metre pocket in the centre. The nets are walked along in the water with a person on each end. The usual sweep is for 15 or 20 minutes and the net is dragged up onto the sand where the catch is sorted.

Legal size mesh on prawn nets is 3 cm which is fairly large and lets a lot of small bait sized prawns through. To increase the catch of small prawns place a bundle of ribbon weed about as big as a football in the pocket of the net before starting to haul the net.

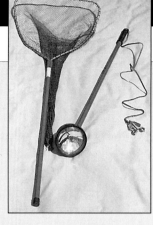

Above: A prawn scoop net and submersible spot light are needed for prawning.
Below: Fine gauge nets can be used for catching shrimp in saltwater and a variety of freshwater baits.

Scoop Nets

Scoop nets or prawn scoops are inexpensive and an effective and easy way to gather bait such as prawns, shrimp and small fish. Together with a strong torch or lantern these nets are all that is needed to take a good haul of prawns from shallow sand flats in estuaries and lakes. The scoop net can also be put to good use around wharves and jetties to take bait fish such as garfish, hardyheads and small yellowtail or squid. Even in daylight hours, a scoop net run through ribbon weed or seagrass areas will often pick up prawns, shrimp and other bait.

Scoop nets have a light, aluminium frame which makes the work easy. Some also come with a longer handle or an extension which can be screwed on if collecting bait fish or prawning from a pier or jetty.

When working with scoop nets it pays to work in pairs. Prawns swimming on the surface are easy to net but prawns feeding on the bottom can be hard to catch.

By working in pairs it is possible to place one net behind the prawn while the other net comes in from the front. By bringing the two nets together the prawn must end up in one of them.

The mesh size on prawn scoops is far smaller than the mesh on prawn drag nets and the scoop net will catch and hold quite small size prawns which can be a distinct advantage when collecting bait.

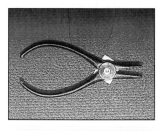

Top: Aerators keep live bait swimming by oxygenating water in containers.
Middle: Plastic worm pliers can help anglers grasp those difficult beach worms.
Bottom: Berley buckets fitted to the stern of boats provide a constant stream of finely chopped fish or bread to attract baitfish.

enter the plastic traps more readily. The netting traps are at their best catching shrimp and small crabs.

The small netting bait bag is baited with fish heads and placed on the edge of thick ribbon weed beds and left overnight. The following morning a good supply of shrimps will be in the trap.

If mullet are required bait both the keeper bag and the inside of the trap with bread and place in the shallows. The mullet will enter the trap if attracted.

The key to the effective trapping of mullet, shrimp, crabs and others is to ensure the funnels of the trap are directly in line with the current flow. These traps only work in calm water situations and are not suited to surf or high current areas.

Home-made traps work just as well as the store bought versions and they are generally easy to make with some screen mesh and a wooden frame.

The Bait Pump

A good bait pump for extracting yabbies, worms and small crabs from estuary flats is an excellent investment when weighed against the frequent purchase of prawns and other bait.

These pumps consist of a round cylinder, usually of non-rusting metal about 60 to 80 cm long and 50 mm in diameter.

Suction is delivered by pulling up a plunger, to the end of which is screwed a series of pliable, rubber

washers which are compressed by a wing nut to make an airtight fit and allow suction. The suction can be adjusted to cope with the different characteristics of sand and mud.

Using a bait pump is a matter of timing. The pump should be pushed into the sand over a yabby or sand worm hole and the plunger withdrawn. When the pump has reached its limit, it is taken from the sand and the plunger pushed down to eject the sand and the trapped yabbies, worms or crabs.

Nippers or bass yabbies are soon exposed as they try to flap and dig their way back into the soft surface.

Because the pump is made from polished metal it is easy to push into the sand and also to pull out.

When working in water where no exposed bank is available for sorting worms or yabbies a sieve is used to catch the bait. These sieves are available from most tackle stores and many anglers place an inner tube around the sieve to make its use in deeper water easy.

Shovel and Pitch Fork

A shovel, spade or fork is useful for digging worms in estuaries. It is hard work but the blood worms extracted make great bait as do any of the worm family.

Some areas are closed to worm digging so check the rules. There are also envi-

Bucket, torch and net are the essentials for catching prawns and other bait at night.

ronmental considerations and it is destructive to dig in weed bed areas. However, rocky, muddy and sandy shores are acceptable areas for digging worms.

Knife

A sturdy bait knife is an essential tool of angling. The only trick is to keep it sharp so it can do the best work when you need it.

Plastic hand spools or corks can be used to rig lines for bait catching.

Sharp, sturdy knives are an essential part of bait preparation.